Psychology

of

Evil

Psychology

of

Evil

THE ORIGIN OF EVIL AT THE PERSONAL LEVEL

KIM MICHAELS

MORE TO LIFE PUBLISHING

www.morepublish.com

For foreign and translation rights,

contact info@ morepublish.com

ISBN: 978-87-93297-00-5

The information and insights in this book should not be considered as a form of therapy, advice, direction, diagnosis, and/or treatment of any kind. This information is not a substitute for medical, psychological, or other professional advice, counseling and care. All matters pertaining to your individual health should be supervised by a physician or appropriate health-care practitioner. No guarantee is made by the author or the publisher that the practices described in this book will yield successful results for anyone at any time. They are presented for informational purposes only, as the practice and proof rests with the individual.

For more information:

www.ascendedmasterlight.com

www.transcendencetoolbox.com

CONTENTS

INTRODUCTION: HOPE FOR TRANSCENDING HUMAN EVIL

It was one of those exhilarating spring days where the sky was so blue that you felt like you could fall right up into it. The newly unfolded leaves were so transparent that you thought they must have come from a better world. The birds were making music that beat the best human composers. I rode my bike to school while taking it all in, and I was filled with the sense that I lived in a world where – although there were surely a few problems here and there – everything was basically good. I had absolutely no idea that my innocent – one might say *naive* – world view was about to be shattered so effectively that it would take me over 20 years to feel like I could make at least some sense out of life.

The first lesson was normal, but then our entire grade level – I was in the eighth grade and 14 years old – was told to go to the auditorium. That usually meant we had to watch some kind of educational movie, meant to scare us away from smoking or enlighten us about the mysteries of oil exploration in the deep sea. As we got seated in the auditorium, everyone was chatting as usual. Some of the boys were hoping for a sex-education movie and making the kind of jokes only teenage boys can find funny. The light was turned off and the movie started rolling. It was black-and-white so obviously one of these "don't do this" kind of movies.

It turned out this was a different kind of movie than I had ever seen in school or on television. It was a movie about the Holocaust and the Nazi death camps. Over the next hour, the screen was filled with the most graphic images possible, and in their stark, black-and-white realism they had a far greater impact than anything today's CSI television shows can muster. Some of the images were burned into my memory so I can still see them on the inside of my eyelids.

There were the cattle cars used to haul unsuspecting people to the camps, the shower heads that gushed out deadly gas instead of water, the piles of human hair and the lamp shades made of human skin with tattoos. There were the living people, some in their striped uniforms, some naked so one could count their ribs. There were the dead people being thrown into piles by soldiers who must have lost all sense of humanity. There were the endless rolls of barb wire on the fence, the towers with machine guns and the crematorium chimneys. The – for me – most high-impact scene was the one in which a door to a crematorium oven swung open and revealed a half-burned skeleton with a wide open mouth, seeming to let out an endless scream: "Whyyyyyyyy?"

After an hour in this black-and-white hell, where I felt chilled to the bone, the light was turned back on, the doors opened and we once again walked out into the warming sunshine. Gone were the sleazy jokes; in fact I don't think anyone said a word. Neither did any of the teachers say a word in the lessons that followed. We were literally shown this absolute horror movie and then expected to go back to a normal school day as if nothing had happened. I distinctly remember noticing that the birds were still singing as if nothing had happened, and for one of the few moments in my life, I wished I was not a human being but a bird having no understanding of man-made horrors.

During my school years, I had quite a few questions about why the Danish school system found it necessary to expose young people to certain things. The biggest question I ever had was what kind of human being can come up with the idea to expose young people to a movie like this with no preparation and – especially – with no follow-up? Yes, of course, we all knew something about the war, but none of us had ever been exposed to anything like what we saw on that spring day. Yes, of course, it was right to educate us about the Holocaust, but this was not education—it was brutal shock therapy.

I have often wondered how anyone could do this and not give us a chance to process the experience, and I have only one plausible answer. The answer is that even after more than 25 years – I saw the movie in 1972 – the Danes who had experienced the war still did not know how to talk about the evils of Nazism. It was considered one of these things that children had to know about when they were old enough. Since the adults didn't know how to talk about evil, they just showed us this movie and felt they had done their duty.

We must find a way to talk about evil

Why am I starting this book by reminiscing about my lost innocence? Because it shows us one of the most prominent aspects of how most people deal with the topic of evil: They don't know how to talk about it, *so they don't!* This is the worst possible reaction because it allows evil to hide. As long as evil can hide, we will continue to live in a world in which events such as the Holocaust, Hiroshima, Stalin's regime, the Cultural Revolution, Pol Pot, Rwanda, human trafficking, child molestation, chemical warfare, land mines and countless other evils will be seen as something we simply can't do anything about.

When you think you can't do anything about an issue, you would rather not talk about it—or even think about it. This is the biggest problem with writing a book about evil: Who wants to read about the topic? Many people are so intimidated by evil that they dare not truly look at the issue. Our first task has now become clear, namely to establish a more constructive foundation for talking about evil. Let me begin by introducing two ideas:

• Albert Einstein said: "If you keep doing the same thing and expect different results, you are insane." For a very long time, we human beings have continued to do the same thing about evil, namely ignoring it. At the same time we have been hoping that one fine day it will go away by itself. Evil hasn't gone away, and that means our approach to evil is a form of collective insanity.

• While we have been largely ignoring evil, we have not been ignoring many more specific problems. Cholera used to be considered a deadly disease and people felt quite powerless about it, meaning they were afraid to talk about it. Then scientists discovered bacteria and realized a specific type of bacteria often found in drinking water is the cause of cholera. Today, cholera is a disease that can be prevented and cured, meaning we can easily talk about it. What is the difference? The difference is that you are only powerless when you don't know the cause of your problem. Once the cause is known, you often see a way to do something about the problem, and now you have a constructive way of talking about possible solutions.

Why is evil still around? It is because we have not yet found a constructive way of talking about evil. We feel powerless because we do not know the cause of evil and we cannot see how to find solutions. Why haven't we discovered the cause of evil? Could it be because we have not been willing to talk openly about it? There is something about evil that seems so intimidating to many people that they prefer not to look. If you don't dare to look, how will you ever discover the cause?

Knowledge is power. We feel powerless to do something about evil because we don't know enough about it. If we decide to make an effort to look more closely at evil, we will learn more about it and this might show us what to do.

In this book and the following book (*A Cosmology of Evil*), I will not only take a look at evil, I will talk about it in a more direct and open manner than it has ever been done before. In this book, I will explore the psychological aspect of evil, and let me explain why that is important.

Why evil has a psychological component

After I had watched the Holocaust movie, I had a burning question in my mind. I simply had to understand how I could be living in a world where such things could happen. For many years, I came no closer to answering this question, and the reason was that I had adopted my society's approach to the problem. I had been brought up to see Adolph Hitler as the ultimate example of an evil person. Denmark is close to

Germany and the Danish people are not all that different from the German people. Yet we Danes were firmly convinced that we could never have been deceived into following Hitler.

The effect was that I had been brought up to do what most people do: We see evil as being somewhere "out there" and as being caused by something that is not in ourselves. As I grew older, this denial became increasingly difficult to sustain. It became completely unsustainable when I started studying the Nazi leaders, the people who had carried out Hitler's orders without questioning them. Even if we still maintain that Hitler himself was a uniquely evil person, it is impossible to think that the hundreds of people around him were also evil.

For example, I learned that the commandant of the Auschwitz death camp, Rudolph Höss, would spend his days overseeing the killing of thousands of Jewish children. After working hours, he would go home to his own family and be an exemplary father to his three children. When I took an honest look at what is known about Höss and many of the other Nazi leaders, it became clear that they were not evil people. They were doing things that most people now see as evil, but they were not evil people. They were firmly convinced that what they were doing was good because it served a noble cause.

I also became aware that while the actions of the Nazi leaders were certainly severe, they were by no means unique. Many people throughout history have committed acts that were clearly evil, yet they themselves were not evil people. What can explain this? Clearly, doing evil while believing you are doing good means that you are blinded by an illusion. We now have two options:

- Certain people are so stupid or gullible that they can easily be deceived into doing evil. The rest of us could never be deceived like this. We can then wash our hands and continue to project that the cause is "out there."

• There is a mechanism in the human psyche – the psyche that all of us share – that makes it possible for us to be deceived into doing evil. We human beings have an ability to do evil while being completely convinced that what we are doing is necessary, perhaps even that it is done in order to bring about a greater good.

If we choose the first option, we are no closer to exposing the cause of evil. If the choose the second one, we might make some progress. We then see that it is only by understanding and unmasking this mechanism that we have a realistic hope of overcoming it. Evil is *not* caused by a hoofed figure in the nether realms or by a few evil people. The very mechanism that allowed Rudolph Höss to oversee the killing of Jewish children during the day while seeing no connection between them and his own children is a psychological mechanism.

There is a unique value in recognizing that the cause of evil behavior is a psychological mechanism. All human beings have a psyche, and that means we need to look inside ourselves for an explanation. This will be uncomfortable at first, but it is ultimately empowering and liberating.

As long as the cause of evil is *outside* ourselves, it follows that we have little power to do anything about it. If the cause is inside ourselves, we might actually have the ability to do something about it. This possibility is precisely what we will explore in this book.

The good and the bad news about evil

The basic premise of this book is that we – meaning you and I – *can* do something about evil. What we can do starts with raising our awareness. Here is the good news about evil:

> When you see evil for what it is, you *will* be free of
> evil—*instantly*. When enough people see evil for
> what it is and speak out about it, the world *will* be
> free from evil—*eventually*.

Before I am labeled as a hopeless idealist, let me give you the bad news about evil:

> In order to see evil for what it is, you have to be
> willing to question *everything*. Because most people
> have "mental holy cows" that they are not willing
> to question, evil will probably be able to hide for a
> while longer.

The importance of recognizing the link between evil and the human psyche is that we can overcome the sense of being powerless. The first thing we can do is to start questioning what has not been questioned in the past. This is cause for hope because we live in an age where more and more people are beginning to question what previous generations saw as unquestionable.

Let us therefore dare to "boldly question what no human has questioned before" by looking at the psychological mechanism that allows us to do evil while being convinced we are doing good.

1 | WHY THE PEOPLE WHO CAN STOP CONFLICT DON'T

"If the Jews destroy the Dome of the Rock, it'll be World War III." I heard these words in a coffee and juice bar in the Old City of Jerusalem, just a few hundred meters from the iconic mosque, the *Dome of the Rock*, that sits on what the Jews believe should be the site of the third and final Jewish temple. They were uttered by an otherwise kind and gentle Palestinian man who served as a free-lance guide for tourists.

The backdrop was that two days earlier a group of Jewish zealots had forced their way into the enclosure around the mosque. They had blockaded the entry, apparently in order to prevent Muslims from getting to their normal prayer service. Within minutes, there had been a gathering of Muslims from the Arab quarter, seeking to forcefully remove the Jews. The Israeli riot police soon appeared and had reportedly arrested many of the Muslims while letting the Jews go home.

This incident points towards the psychological mechanism that is the topic of this book. It also points to the necessity of having the more peaceful people enter public debate. The simple fact is that those who have the potential to change the debate often withdraw from the debate. I will address this problem from several vantage points.

The psychology of compartmentalization

I had been having a pleasant conversation with my Palestinian guide. We could relate as two human beings, recognizing and respecting the humanity in each other. When I made a remark about some Jews wanting to destroy the Mosque in order to build a temple, his countenance changed instantly. It was as if I was now talking to an entirely different person. Whereas before he had recognized the wrongness and futility of war and conflict, he had now shifted into the opposite view.

Because the world had created the state of Israel, it was the world's responsibility to prevent zealous Jews from destroying one of the most holy sites of Islam. If the world did not fulfill this responsibility, then it was only just that the result was a world-wide war. The killing of tens of millions of people was simply the just consequence of the world failing to do what it was supposed to do according to his world view. He was ready to have millions of people killed because of a building that could be destroyed in seconds by an earthquake, something that has hit Jerusalem in the past.

Why was it possible for Rudolph Höss to see no connection between his own children and the Jewish children being pushed into gas chambers or sent to Doctor Mengele for medical experiments? Höss, as my Palestinian guide, had created two compartments in his mind. One compartment had human beings like himself, and the other compartment had non-humans. Neither of these two men – separated by over six decades in time and thousands of kilometers in space

– saw basic humanity in the Jews. If Höss had been ordered by Himmler to send his own children to the gas chambers, he would no doubt have refused. He would have argued that it was wrong – even evil – to kill innocent children. How could he then fail to apply this same standard to the Jewish children being stripped naked outside the gas chambers? He saw the basic humanity in his own children, but he had blocked out the humanity in the Jewish children. He did not believe he was killing human beings.

This ability to create compartments in our minds is clearly part of the mechanism that allows us to do evil with the belief that good will come. In the rest of this book, we will investigate the nature of this mechanism and explore its origin. My immediate aim is to point out why we have not made progress towards transcending human evil.

Why we need a new approach to conflict

We need a new approach to conflict because the one we have taken so far obviously isn't working. If it had been working, we would have manifested a more peaceful world.

I grew up in a relatively peaceful country so it is easy to overlook or forget that we are living on the edge. When I was in Jerusalem and felt the ever-oscillating tension between Jews and Muslims, I realized that human conflict is like an invisible gas that has filled up a mineshaft and is simply waiting for a spark in order to burst forth in a violent explosion. In the Middle East, this tension has existed for thousands of years. There are people who – as a group – simply wouldn't know who they are if they didn't define their group as being in conflict with another group. The explanation is the psychological mechanism that allows us to compartmentalize and label some human beings as non-humans. This also explains why our present approach to conflict is a form of collective insanity. We can divide people into two categories:

- Some people have begun to see through the illusion of compartmentalization. They have started freeing themselves from it and have begun to recognize the basic, universal humanity in all people.

- Some people are still completely blinded by compartmentalization. They are convinced that their view of certain other people as non-humans is justified by some ultimate authority.

If we are to make progress towards overcoming evil, it will require us to free the collective mind from the illusion of compartmentalization. Who can do that? It will not be done by the people who are still blinded by this illusion, meaning it can *only* be done by those who have started to awaken. This is where we run into a mechanism that tends to pacify the people who hold the key to solving the problem:

- While you are blinded by compartmentalization, you are convinced that your world view is right, even the only right one. You think your world view is supported by an ultimate authority. It is necessary for some greater good to force other people to accept your view. You are willing to force others and this makes you quite outspoken and aggressive. You might even be willing to resort to physical force in order to further your cause.

- When you start to awaken, you lose the sense that your world view is the only right one. You see the futility of using force in order to get other people to comply. You become non-aggressive.

As you awaken, you lose the desire to force others but you also develop an aversion to having others force you. This means you simply do not want to deal with the aggressive people, and that is why you want to withdraw from the debate. The result on a world-wide scale is that the very people who have the potential to take humanity beyond compartmentalization withdraw from public debate. The debate is left for the aggressive people and the result is inevitable.

People trapped in compartmentalization divide viewpoints into the one that is right (their own) and all the others that are wrong. They divide people into those who are right (those who agree with them) and those who are wrong. This will inevitably lead to conflict between groups of people espousing different world views.

People blinded by compartmentalization can see only one possible resolution to such conflict, namely that their world view must eradicate all conflicting views. If that means eradicating the people who stubbornly defend wrong views, then this is simply a justifiable means to a superior end.

The conclusion is clear: Those who create conflict will *never* stop conflict. There is an old saying that if good people do nothing, evil will inevitably triumph. We can also say that if the non-aggressive people do not enter public debate, the aggressive people will continue to create conflict until they destroy each other (and perhaps the rest of us in the process).

Having your equilibrium disturbed

Haven't we all looked at the issue of human evil and felt that it was far too much for any of us to deal with? What can "little ol' me" possibly do about such a big problem? How can one person help solve a problem on a global scale?

Most people feel the problem of evil is too big for them so they would rather ignore it. Most of us have found some kind of balance, some sense of equilibrium, that allows us to live in a world where there is evil. This hasn't resolved anything, but it has numbed us to the extent that we can live with the problem. As long as things don't get worse – as long as nothing disturbs the status quo – we will continue to live with the problem without doing anything about it. This sense of equilibrium is one of the greatest enemies of progress because it prevents us from recognizing the following:

- There is a problem, and this is the problem.

- This problem is not normal, it is not the way things need to be.

- If we do nothing, the problem will not only persist but will get worse.

- It is time to do something about the problem.

Before we can recognize a problem, see it for what it is and decide to do something about it, we have to be willing to have our sense of equilibrium disturbed. Why aren't we still living in caves and knocking each other on the head with clubs? What is the underlying mechanism that has allowed the human race to go from the cave man stage to modern civilization in just a few thousand years? The driving force behind all progress is our ability to ask questions, but what we need to question is often the very beliefs that give us a sense of equilibrium. The deciding factor in progress is not our *ability* to ask questions but our *willingness* to question the very beliefs that make us feel comfortable.

People who are still blinded by compartmentalization are not willing to question their world view. We who have started to awaken have been willing to question our world view, but we might have developed a new sense of equilibrium. This is often based on the belief that we simply have to be kind to everyone and then the world will become a better place.

This simply isn't enough. We *do* need to be kind, but it is not true kindness to allow people to live in an illusion without giving them the option to overcome it. The people blinded by compartmentalization will not be free unless someone challenges the illusion. Many of the people who have the potential to do this are so unwilling to have their equilibrium disturbed that they would rather do nothing. I hope this book can help people see that there is a better option.

The approach I will describe does not require us to go out and do battle with the aggressive people. It requires us to challenge the illusion of compartmentalization and the psychological mechanism that allows people to do evil while thinking they are doing good. If those of us who *can* do this refuse to do so, then evil will indeed continue to dominate life on this planet.

Why we need non-aggressive people

Albert Einstein is also famous for another quote: "You can't solve a problem with the same state of consciousness that created the problem." Many non-aggressive people have a dream of one day seeing a more peaceful world. Perhaps we even have visions of a golden-age society where conflict, poverty and starvation are unknown. We know that in order for this peaceful society to come about, humanity must transcend its present level of consciousness, but this is where we stop. There is a gap between our vision of a peaceful world and our vision of how it might come about. The reason for this gap is a psychological mechanism that we need to wrestle with.

The aggressive people are the ones who create most conflicts. Because they are aggressive, they are also the ones who think they can run society and solve all problems. The non-aggressive people do not generate conflict, but that also means we tend to walk away from situations where there is conflict. When the aggressive people take over the debate, we who are the non-aggressive people tend to withdraw, leaving it to the aggressive people to deal with the problem.

When it comes to the issue of resolving human conflict, who are the people that step forward to have a go at it? It is either the very same people who generated the conflict, or it is people with the same aggressive mindset as the ones who generated the conflict. Humanity has so far been attempting to solve the problem of human conflict with the exact same mindset that created the problem. This is a completely dysfunctional dynamic, and it can never lead to a peaceful world. If there ever is to be "peace on earth and good will among men—and *women*," this dysfunctional dynamic must be changed.

Do you think the aggressive people will one day wake up and decide they have had enough of conflict? They might, but I have decided that I am not going to wait for that to happen. Instead, I have acknowledged that if we are to create a peaceful world, we who are the non-aggressive people need to stop running away from public debate. We need to step forward—not by doing what the aggressive people are doing but by providing an alternative to their aggressive mindset. We need to call for a new approach, we need to be like the little boy who cried out: "But the emperor has nothing on!"

If we, the non-aggressive people, don't enter the debate, the dynamic will not change and the outcome will be the same. We who are the non-aggressive people need to realize that if we continue to do the same thing – allowing the aggressive people to dominate the debate – and at the same time expect different results – expect that those who create conflict can overcome conflict – then we are the ones who are insane.

I have decided to stop doing the same thing. I have decided to speak out and explore a new approach to the issue of evil, and I am sharing that approach in this book. Will you at least contemplate this approach and see whether it might inspire you to stop "doing the same thing?" If you feel that some of my thoughts resonate with you, then let us see if we, together, can produce a different result on this planet.

2 | NON-AGGRESSIVE PEOPLE CAN MAKE A DIFFERENCE

Given that most conflicts are started by people with an aggressive approach to life and given that these people also tend to think they are the ones who can solve all of humankind's problems, is it even possible for the non-aggressive people to have any impact on society's approach to evil? Is there any realistic hope that the non-aggressive people can make a difference? If so, how might we make a difference?

A revolutionary view of history

Most of us were brought up with a pacifying view of history. We were told that historical change comes about as the result of certain forces over which most people have no control. This may be natural laws, sociological factors, the decisions of kings or emperors or even the unpredictable stroke of genius in rare individuals.

Common for all of these factors is that ordinary people have no influence on history. We are members of the big, unnamed masses of humanity. We are like jellyfish in the ocean, passively moving along with the prevailing currents. All we can do is stand by and watch as impersonal forces or the ruling elite bring about historical change. It definitely isn't brought about by us and we don't even make any contribution to change. We are mere spectators in the theater of history.

Let me challenge that view of history by giving two examples. The first one is slavery. For thousands of years, virtually every culture had slaves. Slavery was taken for granted and it wasn't even questioned in most cultures. During the 18th and 19th century, Western civilization gradually began to debate and eventually outlaw slavery. Why did this happen? It certainly wasn't brought about by the ruling elite.

The "common" people did not have slaves. Slaves were owned by the elite, the rich and the mighty who are – according to the way I was taught history – the ones who bring about change in society. They were the ones who owned slaves and the reason was simple: They had an economic incentive. What is better from an economic viewpoint than being able to harvest the fruits of other people's labor for the minimal cost of keeping them alive? Nothing happened during the 1700s that took away the economic incentive for owning slaves. The incentive for slavery was greater than ever because of the industrial revolution that was based on manual labor. The less you had to pay for labor, the greater your profit.

Slavery was not abolished because of a change in economic conditions, and it was not abolished by the elite—they were the ones with the economic incentive for keeping it alive. Slavery was abolished because of a shift in the way Western people were looking at themselves. This shift made it clear that human beings are more than mere objects, and thus they cannot be bought or sold as property. No one can own another human being because each human being is a distinct individual that is endowed with certain rights—rights that no other human being has the right to take away!

This shift did not take place somewhere "out there" in some mystical realm beyond our reach. It took place "in here," namely in the mind or psyche of individuals within society. The change was started by a few individuals, such as philosophers who started writing about new ideas. Yet the changes were not brought about by these philosophers and they were not brought about by the ruling elite.

The changes happened because a growing number of people among the general population became aware of the new ideas and began to accept them, speaking out in favor of them. This happened slowly and gradually, but at some point a critical mass was reached and there was a shift in society. The ruling elite realized that they could no longer ignore the new ideas—or the population might actually revolt. This seems to be something the ruling elite fears.

Why democracy is a most revolutionary idea

The abolishment of slavery cannot be understood as an isolated event. It was part of a larger trend that brought about other changes, the most dramatic of which is democracy. My second example of how historical change happens is the switch from various forms of totalitarian governments to a democratic form of government. This is a truly revolutionary change, far more revolutionary than most of us were taught in history class.

For thousands of years, virtually every society – with a brief exception in ancient Greece – was ruled by a small elite who had near absolute power over the general population. The population had to live within the boundaries defined by the ruling elite, and they had no way of improving their lives beyond what was allowed by the elite. If the elite required them to give free labor or to give military service in the elite's incessant drive for conquest, the people had no right to say "No!" For the greater part of human history, the general population have been the slaves of a small elite.

Human history is a constant battle where the general population is seeking greater freedom whereas various elite groups are seeking to restrict freedom in order to secure power and privileges for themselves. History is a battle between two opposing forces, freedom and slavery, rights and power. This battle is personified by an elite whose members constantly seek greater power and privilege by taking freedom and rights from the majority of the population. The British historian Arnold Toynbe talked about a dominant minority who is seeking to control the population and a creative minority who is seeking to bring forth ideas and inventions that free the population. The deciding factor is neither the dominant nor the creative minority. The deciding factor is always the majority.

The majority of the population have one strength—they are the majority. A ruling elite is by its nature limited in numbers because it consists of self-centered people who do not want to share. Members of the elite cannot by themselves suppress the population through force.

The totalitarian governments seen throughout history give some pretty radical examples of how a small elite had managed to suppress and control a large population. If the population had been united in opposing the elite, then the elite would always lose. This is simply a matter of adding up the numbers. Hitler and his Nazi party bosses would have lost power in five minutes if the German people had refused to comply. The SS and the Gestapo simply could not have arrested everyone, and eventually they would have refused to arrest their own family members. Hitler would have been Führer by name only for no one would have followed him.

It was a momentous revolutionary shift from societies ruled by a power elite to societies with a democratic form of government. It was a complete break with 5,000 years of history! Instead of allowing a small elite to rule them, the population now demanded to have a direct influence on their societies and their destiny. Instead of accepting a society based on the principle that "might is right," the population now demanded a society based on the concept that each human being has rights that no other human being – not even an emperor, king, Führer or pope – can take away from them.

A shift in the psyche

What drove this change was a shift in people's awareness and understanding. It was a shift in the psyche, even the collective psyche. It started with a few people who accepted the idea of rights, and this acceptance gradually grew until a critical mass was reached. Then the members of the ruling elite were faced with a simple choice. They could resist democracy and risk another French revolution in their nation, or they could give way for a democratic form of government. There were, of course, other options, as witnessed by the Bolshevik revolution in Russia that did not give the people more freedom or by the fascist revolutions in Europe. Nevertheless, the driving force behind historical change is not *external* forces but *internal* forces. The real cause of historical change is to be found in the human psyche. What drives change in society is a change in consciousness!

Once you see that all change in society begins with a change in the individual and collective consciousness, it becomes obvious that all positive changes started with just a few people who raised their awareness of an issue. We, the non-aggressive people, can make a real contribution by educating ourselves and raising our awareness about the hidden cause of evil. Even by doing this, we will make a difference, as that is how historical change starts. We can, of course, do more by also speaking out about the real cause of evil, thereby contributing to building the critical mass that will inevitably bring about a shift in humankind's approach to conflict.

We, the non-aggressive people, *can* make a difference, and it is proven by the fact that we already have. Who brought about democracy, an end to slavery and greater economic opportunity for all? It certainly wasn't the members of the ruling elite who wanted to maintain the status quo with themselves in privileged positions. Instead, the non-aggressive people were among the first to recognize the validity of human rights. As they continued to speak out about it, the general population eventually caught on. We who are the non-aggressive people of today have a unique opportunity to generate a similar shift in humankind's awareness about the cause of evil. History – correctly understood – is on our side.

Our drive to be more

Even in totalitarian societies, an elite cannot control a large population through physical force alone. It simply cannot be done because of the difference in numbers. The only way for an elite to control the population is to make the population believe in a limited world view that defines boundaries for their own power. This can make the people believe that there is no way for them to change the status quo and free themselves from the elite.

This can be accomplished in various ways. For example, the people of ancient Rome believed they lived in the most sophisticated civilization ever. The people of Medieval Europe believed they would go to hell if they questioned Catholic doctrine—and the power structure of the clergy, the noble class and the king that it supported. The people of Nazi Germany either believed Hitler would lead them to the promised land or that they had no power to rise up against him. A totalitarian society is based on getting the people to accept a limited view of life, which makes them believe there is no realistic alternative to the status quo.

We accept limitations because we believe there is no alternative. We see no alternative because we have a limited understanding of life, a limited perspective. We overcome that limited understanding by asking questions that go beyond our current world view, our current mental box. Once we have a higher understanding, we see that there is indeed an alternative to our limited way of life. When we see the alternative, we will no longer accept our former limitations. If we know we can have a better life, we will want that better life. If people *know* better, they will *do* better.

The medieval feudal societies were text-book examples of elitist societies. A very small power elite consisting of the kings, the noble class and the Catholic clergy controlled 98 percent of the population. They did this for centuries because the Catholic Church had suppressed information to such an extent that the population saw no alternative to their way of life. One aspect of this suppression was the burning of books by the Greek philosophers who talked about a more free and democratic society. These works were preserved by Muslim settlers in Spain, and from here they were reintroduced into European society and led to the renaissance, the scientific revolution and the emergence of democratic ideals.

The population only accepted the limitations of the feudal societies because they saw no alternative. Once the knowledge of an alternative gained widespread acceptance, a critical mass started building and eventually a change occurred. This is precisely the mechanism that will make it possible for a few non-aggressive people to bring about a new approach to evil and conflict.

For thousands of years, we have accepted that our personal relationships and our societies are dominated by conflict and power plays. The simple reason is that we have not seen a realistic alternative. If people saw a realistic way to bring about a peaceful world, the majority would want it as they wanted democracy.

We have seen no alternative to conflict because we have not fully understood the causes of conflict. The reason being that we haven't asked sufficiently creative questions. Who can begin a new movement of asking such questions and bringing them into the public debate, thereby bringing about a shift in public awareness that – once critical mass is reached – *will* bring about a change in society? It is those people who have a non-aggressive approach to life and who are willing to step out of the role of being passive spectators—instead choosing to take an active, but non-violent, role in the public debate.

Although this is a revolutionary view of historical change, there is an even deeper understanding of what brings about change in society. By looking at it, we will also set a better foundation for understanding the cause of evil.

3 | WHY WE THINK WE ARE POWERLESS

We can now identify three main groupings in society:

- **The dominant minority or the power elite.** These people do not form one large, coherent conspiracy, but they do tend to pull society toward a totalitarian form of government. They want to rule, and they believe they are the people most fit for the task. They also tend to believe might is right and that the end can justify the means. They do not want a society based on principles or rights because these cannot easily be manipulated in order to give power and privileges to a small elite.

- **The creative minority of non-aggressive or peaceful people.** These people do believe in principles and universal rights. They have no desire to exercise power over others, nor do they have a desire for inordinate privileges for themselves. These people tend to pull society towards a form of government based on rights and principles, democracy being the natural outcome of this process.

- **The majority of the population.** These people are focused on their personal lives and have limited interest in the broader questions relating to society. Some people have no special veneration for rights but will follow a totalitarian leader if he makes the right promises and seems able to deliver. Others are able to think beyond their daily lives and clearly see the need for a society based on rights and principles.

Neither the dominant nor the creative minority can change society on their own—they both need the compliance or backing of the majority. The deciding factor in how a society evolves is whether the majority of the people follow the dominant minority or the creative minority. The further we go back in time, the more likely it was that the majority would follow a dominant elite. As humankind's knowledge and understanding has grown, the majority is beginning to see through the power plays of the dominant elites and are looking for a different kind of leadership.

The problem is that there is often no alternative to the dominant minority because the members of the creative minority refuse to enter politics and play any kind of power games. Many of the creative, non-aggressive people feel powerless when it comes to making a positive difference in society. We look at the aggressive people and we refuse to fight or work with them, partly because we do not want to play their power games and partly because we refuse to compromise our principles. In many cases, compromise seems to be necessary in order to get along in politics.

History clearly seems to be moving society towards a greater and greater understanding, which causes the majority to want a more enlightened form of leadership. Why do the non-aggressive people still feel powerless? Why do so many people – especially the non-aggressive people who *can* offer an alternative to conflict – feel powerless to change society—is it possible we were brought up to feel powerless?

We are children of a war between belief systems

A few years ago, I read a report about the psychological effects that children experience after having been through a physical war. One of them is that they do tend to feel powerless. They have directly experienced that their lives were shattered by events over which they had no control. They are unable to trust that this will not happen again, giving them a passive approach to life. They feel powerless to affect changes on a large scale.

After reading this, I realized that I too am a child of war and so is just about anyone else who has grown up in modern, Western civilization. I am not talking about a physical war but the fact that our civilization has a schizophrenic approach to the deeper questions of life. As young children most of us were exposed to the war between fundamentally incompatible world views. There was nothing we could do to avoid this conflict, and we were far too young to be able to deal with it without being wounded. Although we were not exposed to a physical war, we were nevertheless exposed to a conflict that we had to deal with, yet most of us received little help in how to put together a coherent world view.

I am specifically talking about the war between scientific materialism and orthodox or mainstream Christianity. This war

deals with what we might call the fundamental questions of life
(who am I, why am I here, where did I come from, does life
have a purpose?). Few children are completely untouched by
these questions, but the creative or non-aggressive people were
deeply touched by this war of ideas. We are non-aggressive
because we are open to the importance of ideas. To us, ideas
are far more powerful than raw force—the pen is mightier than
the sword. Unfortunately, our upbringing directly challenged
this belief. We were exposed to a society that cannot even
decide which ideas are the most important. The war between
ideas has to a large degree neutralized the influence of ideas—
leaving our societies to be dominated by the more aggressive
people (even if they appear in a democratic framework).

There is a basic human need that is not generally recognized
by society. We human beings need a psychological foundation
in order to function normally. As part of this foundation, we
need to have some understanding of what life is about and
how it works. We need a basic world view as a foundation for
our interaction with "life," including society and other people.

What do we get? We get a schizophrenic world view that
is dominated by two opposing camps, each of which is claiming the other is fundamentally wrong. Anyone with a basic IQ
can see that the two opposing views are incompatible—they
simply cannot both be right. What is a child to do at the age of
six, eight or ten or whenever this basic conflict intrudes upon
our innocent minds? Can we be expected to resolve what the
adults who run our society have not been able to resolve? Can
we be expected to make sense out of this? Obviously not, so
what do we do? Well, let's look at the three groups mentioned
above:

- People in the dominant minority have a very simple reaction to any situation where there is a conflict

between two sides. They pick one side, elevate it to the status of superiority and then focus all of their energy on fighting to destroy the opposing side. They believe society will be better off if their side wins.

• Among the broader population, some people follow the dominant minority and pick one side. The better educated a society becomes, the more people among the population start questioning the black-and-white approach that one side is completely right and the other completely wrong. The general tendency is that people will either follow one of the competing power elite groups or take a passive approach.

• The creative minority are creative precisely because they see beyond the black-and-white approach. Instead of siding with one of the competing sides, we tend to look for a deeper understanding of life. This causes many of us to go on a personal journey for greater understanding and meaning, and we often take decades to find a new approach. This also makes us reluctant to force our personal approach upon others, which then tends to make us take a passive approach to speaking out in the public debate.

Once again, the debate is left to be dominated by the aggressive people. We who are the creative minority tend to step back, and so do the more aware people among the general population. Since there seems to be no alternative to having society led by the aggressive people, a majority among the population simply lose interest in politics and step back. This is exactly what the dominant minority wants to see happen. You may never have considered the existence of a power elite

whose members know that they can only continue to dominate society by pacifying the majority and especially the creative elite. Obviously, we were not taught about the existence
of such an elite.

Why weren't we taught this—given that a democratic society supposedly is created to prevent a small elite from controlling the population? One would think a democratic society
would want to educate its citizens to the potential for the
emergence of a dominant elite that can undermine democracy.
Does the fact that democratic societies do not educate people
about this problem prove that there *is* an elite, and that this
elite has managed to influence our democratic societies in subtle ways?

In a totalitarian society, might is to some degree right. In
a democratic society, knowledge is right because people can
only vote based on what they know. If you can control information, you can control how people vote—or discourage the
more informed people from voting because they can see that
all candidates will maintain status quo.

My actual aim is to help you feel less powerless, and by
talking about a power elite that controls society behind the
scenes, I have probably – at least if the topic is new to you
– caused you to feel even more powerless. I have done this
because in order to move beyond feeling powerless, we have
to take a look at the factors that make us feel powerless. Once
we understand what we are up against, we can begin to do
something about it. It is likely that when the first scientists
discovered bacteria and realized they can cause disease, they
at first felt quite powerless. As they began to understand how
bacteria work, they could see ways to kill harmful bacteria and
thus new opportunities for curing disease opened up.

What determines our willingness to ask questions?

The discrepancies between various belief systems is one of the major causes of large-scale conflict. Millions of people have been killed in wars between competing religions or competing political systems. Is the conflict between belief systems truly inherent or unavoidable?

Throughout history, we do see that different belief systems or world views can co-exist without creating violent conflict. For example, during the 1400s, an area in Southern Spain, called Al Andalus, saw the peaceful co-existence of Muslims, Jews and Christians, and as a result the community was thriving in all ways. In the East, various religions, such as Hinduism, Buddhism and Taoism have coexisted peacefully for centuries.

Human beings have always had a variety of belief systems or world views. It is not the difference in beliefs that in itself causes conflict. The real cause of conflict is when we start approaching our beliefs in a specific way. The people who cause conflict are those who feel threatened by the existence of belief systems that are different from their own. How can we explain that some people feel a need to forcefully suppress or destroy ideas that conflict their own belief system?

One way to explain this is to say, as many modern psychologist do, that there are two basic human emotions, namely love and fear:

- If your personal psychology is dominated by love, you tend to be curious about life. You are less prone to believe that one belief system is the absolute one and can give you all of the knowledge you need or are allowed to have.

- If your psychology is dominated by fear, you are not curious about other belief systems. You want the sense of security or even superiority that comes from thinking that your belief system is in some way superior to all others.

Given that the driving force behind progress is our willingness to ask questions outside our current mental box, the more love and curiosity you have, the more willing you are to ask such creative questions. The more you are dominated by fear, the more you want to suppress any question beyond the mental box defined by your infallible belief system.

I still remember my utter shock when as a child I learned that there was a time when most people in the Western world believed the earth was flat. Even the most intelligent people in society believed the earth was a flat disc. I just couldn't believe it, and it took me several decades before I came to understand the underlying psychological mechanism. Our ability to ask questions is counteracted by another "ability." This is our desire for psychological stability or security.

Consider the immense distance we have traveled from the stone age to modern civilization. This journey has taken us through innumerable questions, but the journey has not been a steady progression. There have been historical periods in which our ability to ask questions was seriously confined by our desire for security. This need to have a firm foundation for our outlook on life has caused us to create belief systems and then reason that such systems could explain everything we *needed* to know—or were *allowed* to know.

Certain questions become "forbidden questions," meaning we are not allowed to ask them. If we do ask these questions, we might be persecuted by some human authority. I was completely shocked when I heard about the Inquisition, the burning of books and the persecution of early scientists. Our questions might also make us vulnerable to the ultimate form of evil—the devil himself. There have been periods when asking questions about evil was seen as opening your mind to the control of evil forces. We can now identify two contradictory forces working in human psychology:

• There is our built-in curiosity that drives us to ask ever-more creative questions. This ability has driven all progress and has empowered us to find solutions to many problems, giving us the hope that we can solve any problem by asking more creative questions.

• There is the need for security that causes us to create a mental box that supposedly contains all we need to know. Once we have accepted such a mental box as absolute – which our need for security drives us to do – it has literally become a psychological straightjacket that prevents us from asking questions beyond certain boundaries. We are afraid to think outside the box.

Let us now consider how this relates to our three groups, namely the dominant minority, the creative minority and the majority of the population:

• The people who refuse to ask questions and who seek to establish one belief system as superior are the members of the power elite.

• The people who are the most willing to ask questions beyond existing belief systems are the creative minority.

- As time moves on, more and more people among the general population also open their minds to new perspectives.

There has never been a time when there has been a greater opportunity for the members of the creative elite to have a positive impact on society. At the same time, we have never had better opportunities for disseminating new information, especially since the advent of the Internet. We who are the peaceful people have a unique opportunity for making a positive contribution to a more peaceful world.

How belief systems can be used to pacify us

There are two basic approaches to life, one that is dominated by fear and one that is dominated by curiosity. Here is how this relates to people's approach to belief systems:

- If your approach to life is dominated by fear, you have to try to find a way to keep your fear at bay so you can live with it. Most people do this by adopting a belief system and then elevating it to the status of authority, superiority or even infallibility. Once people have done this, they will inevitably feel threatened by another belief system that makes a similar claim. Because the claims are mutually exclusive, it is obvious they cannot both be right, and thus we see the appearance of the need to suppress or destroy a competing belief system. It is not the belief systems themselves that cause conflict but a specific psychological reaction.

• When your approach to life is dominated by curiosity, you have no need to elevate a particular belief system to some ultimate status. Your curiosity drives you to continually seek for a deeper understanding, and you have no need to believe that a particular system has already defined all of the knowledge you *can* have or are *allowed* to have. You may use a system as a foundation for organizing your thoughts, but you never allow a system to become a closed mental box. You also see no conflict between your system and any other system, even if they make contradictory claims. Instead of one system having to destroy another, you realize that some future discovery could lead us beyond all existing systems. You refuse to spend your attention on fighting other systems but instead focus on expanding human knowledge.

Let me now define how I see the two dominant belief systems of Western civilization. When I talk about orthodox or mainstream Christianity, I am referring not to a specific church but to any and all churches or sects that take the fear-based approach to life. This causes people to make absolutist claims about the superiority of their religion or the superiority of their beliefs over a scientific world view. The Catholic Church of the Middle Ages is a textbook example of such an absolutist belief system. The Church claimed to be the only true church of Christ and the only doorway to the kingdom of God. It had the military power to suppress all competing beliefs, and it did so very aggressively, as witnessed by the burning of books, the Crusades, the Inquisition and the suppression of scientists. This is a matter of taking an honest look at the historical record.

What I call scientific materialism is also an absolutist and closed belief system. I make a distinction between science and materialism. By its very nature, science is not a belief system but an open-ended process of continually – and perhaps indefinitely – seeking to expand our understanding of every aspect of life. In its pure form, science cannot conflict a religious belief system because pure science never makes the kind of absolutist claims made by closed religious systems. In its pure form, science can never become a closed mental box because the very essence of science is that there is always more to discover than what we know right now.

Science started out as an open-ended process and not a closed system. The early scientists – from Gallileo to Newton – saw no inherent conflict between science and religion (which was because they also saw religion as an open-ended process, namely mysticism). Over a period of time, a distinct shift started to occur. The field of interpreting scientific discoveries began to be dominated by people who took the fear-based approach to life. These people saw themselves in opposition to the religious authorities, and they now began to portray religion as the cause of conflict. Science could provide us with objective knowledge and thus take us out of the realm of religious superstition and hostility. Science – as a open-ended process of discovery – was hijacked by people who had clear political objectives, namely to reform society in specific ways. The open-ended process of science was pushed in the background, and instead an absolutist system was created. This system was created in order to compete with and replace the absolutist religious systems.

In reality, science was started by the creative minority. As science began to have more impact on society, a grouping within the dominant minority saw the possibility of using science to take power away from the people who ran the religious establishments. This is a pattern found throughout history, namely that an aspiring power elite will take an idea brought forth by the creative minority and use it to take power away from the established power elite. In so doing, the aspiring power elite will often claim to be working for the freedom of the people, but in reality they will limit that freedom once they have dethroned the old elite and put themselves in power. The Bolshevik revolution is the text-book example.

Scientific materialism makes absolutist claims that cannot be verified by science and thus would never be made by a pure scientist. As an example of such absolutist claims, take the claim that there is no God because there is nothing beyond the material universe. No true scientist could make this claim. All one can say as a scientist is that science has found no factual, material evidence of a God. One cannot rule out that new and better methods could be discovered that would allow science to verify the existence of something beyond the material universe (how can material instruments detect something non-material?).

What materialism claims is that there is not, nor could there ever be, anything beyond what is called the material universe—and which is defined as what can be detected by current instruments and methods. This is clearly a political claim deliberately designed to erode people's belief in the – equally absolutist – claims made by religion. Scientific materialism is simply another absolutist belief system, seeking to replace the absolutist system of religion.

Why we were brought up to feel powerless

I earlier said we were brought up to feel powerless, and we can now see why. We grew up in a society that is a battleground between two absolutist belief systems, yet both of them portray us – the ordinary human beings – as essentially powerless creatures:

• According to Christianity, we are sinners by birth or by nature. We were created by a supernatural being who resides in a kingdom that is beyond the material universe (and doesn't have the problems we encounter on earth). This God is supposedly benevolent, meaning that he wants us to come home to his kingdom. This benevolent God created us in a state that makes it impossible for us to enter his kingdom. We need the assistance of a force outside ourselves, a force that can absolve us of the sins that keep us outside the kingdom. That force is supposedly the sacrifice of God's son, but we still need the external religion in order to receive this grace. We have no power on our own to qualify ourselves for entry into the kingdom. We need both an external supernatural force and an external earthly organization in order to enter this higher state.

• Scientific materialism claims that all this is simply superstition, and it seeks to set our minds free from the oppression of absolutist religious institutions. What kind of self-image has materialism given us to replace the concept that we are *sinners* by nature? It has given us the image that we are *animals* by nature. There is no God that cares about us. There are no conscious, self-aware beings beyond ourselves. We are only self-aware due to some fluke of nature. We are the products of a completely unconscious and random process. The fact that we can do things that – other – animals cannot do is not part of some grand plan. It is simply a random product of a process over which we have absolutely no control. When you consider the amazing progress from past societies to modern civilization, you can also see an incredible progression in human thought. According to materialism, our thoughts are not part of some purposeful evolutionary process. They are random products of our genes and the electromagnetic processes in your brains. There is no such thing as a soul, let alone a collective soul or consciousness, that can purposefully progress over time.

Both of the dominant belief systems portray us as fundamentally limited – and thus powerless – beings. Religion says we are sinners because of the fall of Adam and Eve so we are inherently limited by our origin. Science says we are evolved animals, limited by our genes and our upbringing—thus also limited by the past. Even though materialists claim to have freed us from the superstition of religion, they have simply replaced one set of limitations with another. If you take either system at its face value, "we the people" are inherently limited beings, and that of course, inevitably leads us to another reason we were brought up to see ourselves as powerless: Someone wants to control us.

4 | ELITISM IS THE MISSING LINK IN HISTORY

If we take an out-of-the-box look at history, we can discover a tendency that none of us were taught in history class. Most of the large conflicts of history were not caused by the general population but by various elite groups. For example, the Napoleonic wars were not started because the French people had a strong desire to dominate the world. They were started because a small elite in French society – led by Napoleon – had a strong desire to take over the world. Likewise, the German people might have been swept along by Hitler's rhetoric, but is was only a small elite in Germany that started World War II. In every historical period we have seen the existence of various elite groups, and the cause of most conflicts has been the competition or rivalry between such groups. The people have often been dragged into such conflicts but have never initiated them.

There is also an underlying struggle between elite groups and the population. The elite groups have sought to dominate society. Because they are always a small minority, they can accomplish something only by getting the broader population to support their aims. In most cases, that means the elite groups have to restrict the freedoms or rights of the general population. Behind all other conflicts is an underlying struggle between the people who long for freedom and various elite groups who long for power—and will use it to take away the freedom of the people.

There is always a basic tension in any society. A dominant minority forms the established power elite, namely the people who control the dominant institutions in society, such as the political apparatus, the major religion, the financial institutions or the military. One or more aspiring power elite groups are constantly seeking to get a slice of the pie by taking power from the established power elite—perhaps even by generating a revolution whereby they use the people to overthrow the old elite.

The members of the established power elite have managed to attain power by getting the population to accept certain restrictions of their freedom. In the past, this has sometimes been accomplished by force alone, but the most efficient way for a power elite to stay in power is through a combination of force and ideas. For example, the medieval feudal societies survived for centuries because the dominant elite (the kings, the noble class and the Catholic leaders) used a combination of force and religious doctrines to make the population feel powerless. The leaders of the dominant elite are always seeking to suppress any ideas that can empower the population to rise above the limitations that make them feel they cannot live without the elite. Members of the power elite are always seeking to suppress the creative minority or any members of the population who take a stand against their oppression.

History shows that if only a few people challenge the elite, they will often be dealt with decisively, usually by execution.

When sufficient numbers of people take a stand, the power elite will in most cases back down. If enough people stand up, the elite will always have to back down. This can be seen in numerous cases where a popular uprising overturned a dominant elite.

The tension between a power elite and the general population is present even in today's democracies. We are not here talking some far-flung conspiracy theory. We are simply talking about the spontaneous and usually unconscious formation of a dominant elite whose members believe they are better suited for running society than the general population. Such an elite will – not necessarily deliberately – promote ideas that support the existence of an elite and thus make the people feel powerless. Even in our modern democracies, "we the people" have been brought up – partly because of the war between Christianity and materialism – to see ourselves as powerless. As a result, we tend to think there is nothing we can do to help resolve such huge problems as conflict or evil.

Who are the people that make up various power elite groups? They are in almost all cases people whose psychologies are dominated by a fear-based approach to life. The power elite groups are seeking to control others, and the need to control others can only spring from fear. People who tend to take a fear-based approach seek systems that they can elevate to some ultimate status, and this can only create irreconcilable conflicts.

Once again, we see that if there is ever to be any real advance towards overcoming human evil, it will not come from the power elite groups or from anyone else taking a fear-based approach to life. Such people will cling to their systems and seek to defend them to the death. Any real progress can come only from people who do not take a fear-based approach, whether such people belong to a creative minority or to groups who are not afraid to acknowledge their curiosity about life. In order for us to even get started on making a difference, we have to decide to take back our power and rise above the programming that seeks to make us accept ourselves as powerless beings who should let the elite rule society.

Non-aggressive people have already had a major impact on society by setting the stage for the emergence of democracy, the abolishment of slavery, environmental awareness, the need for social justice and many other causes. There is only one realistic conclusion: Regardless of how we might feel as individuals, we are not powerless. We feel powerless because we were brought up to feel powerless. This happened because even our democratic societies have various power elite groups that have a direct interest in making the general population and the creative minority feel powerless—thereby leaving it to them to run society.

I am not hereby saying that the ruling elite is made up of evil people who are part of some grandiose conspiracy. I believe most of the members of the power elite are well-meaning people. They are also people who take a fear-based approach to life, and their fear has distorted – as we will discuss later – their view of life. They think they are doing the right thing, but their fear prevents them from seeing the solution to the problems created by their fear.

The real cause of large-scale conflict is the existence of a dominant minority whose power is based on limiting people's vision and knowledge. If the population knew they could have a better society, they would want it, and that would threaten the dominance of the elite. The elite is not a coherent group, and it has competing factions. In some cases, an aspiring power elite group has claimed to work for the freedom of the people, only to use the people in overthrowing the established power elite. In some cases, such an aspiring elite have even used members of the creative minority, only to discard them once the old elite was overthrown.

These kinds of power plays are the reason we, who are the non-aggressive people, do not want to mess with politics. Yet we do not have to engage in such power plays. I am not seeking to encourage the formation of a group that can oppose the established power elite of our society. My aim is to show that there is an obvious alternative to engaging in a power struggle. We – the non-aggressive people – do not have to fight the aggressive people. We only have to expose them so that a majority of the population will refuse to follow them and refuse to passively let them get away with their power plays.

Knowledge is power. All real progress has been driven by an expansion of knowledge and understanding. This has been brought about by the creative minority, people like ourselves who have a love-based, curious approach to life. We have this option and it truly *can* produce change in society. Once you see this, all sense of being powerless should evaporate as the morning dew under a rising sun. In the next chapter, I will discuss a hidden mechanism that makes it even clearer how a few people can bring about change—positive or negative. The power elite groups have known about this mechanism for centuries, and it is about time the rest of us became aware of it too.

5| ALL PEOPLE ARE CONNECTED

There is an old saying: "History is written by the winners." Those who win a conflict will write history in such a way that it makes themselves look good or promotes their ongoing agenda. Every society has had its power elite groups, and the collective agenda of such groups is to ensure the survival of elitism—a form of society in which a small elite can rule and secure special privileges for themselves. I am not saying there is a conscious conspiracy behind elitism, as the elite consists of many different groups that are in constant rivalry with each other. This rivalry is precisely what prevents the emergence of one dominant group. I am not in the one extreme that says there is a small group that controls the world behind the scenes. Neither do I belong in the opposite extreme that denies all existence of elite groups that are seeking to expand their power and control.

For most of known history, all societies have had power elite groups, and they have attempted to write history to make themselves look good. In so doing, they have written history from their basic mindset, which is that elitism is a force for good and that the members of the elite are the ones who drive historical change. The real cause of historical change has been largely overlooked in the official history books most of us were exposed to in school.

The real cause of change in society is the general population. If they follow the dominant minority, a society moves towards totalitarianism, and this usually leads to a violent conflict with other totalitarian regimes. If the majority follows the creative elite, a society moves towards greater freedom and rights for all people, such as seen in the emergence of democracy. The real cause of historical change is not one or more elite groups but what we might call the "collective consciousness" of the people. A new idea emerges and gradually gains prominence in the minds of the people, until a critical mass is reached and the idea now generates actual change in society.

How do ideas spread?

What has caused us to progress to our present stage is that we ask questions and expand our knowledge. There is a correspondence between curiosity and progress. For example, during what is often called the "Dark Ages," the Catholic Church was successful in suppressing any knowledge that could question its "infallible" doctrines. Public curiosity – people's ability and willingness to ask questions – was rather low. This is why society stagnated and there was little progress for centuries. The same has happened to other repressive regimes that have restricted the population's access to information or their ability to freely discuss ideas.

Why did the Soviet Union collapse? In 1987 I heard a lecture by a Soviet dissident who said that at that time, the greatest problem for the Soviet regime was whether to allow their scientists to have computers. If they *did not,* the Soviet Union would inevitably fall behind the West in terms of scientific progress and weapons development. If they *did* allow the scientists to have computers, they could not control the information scientists could access and disseminate. This could lead to a political collapse—the collapse that did in fact happen only a few years later.

How do ideas actually spread? Does it only happen by individuals studying them and talking or writing about them? Or is there a larger mechanism that can affect the population as a whole?

Every day, when you use the Internet, turn on your television, walk down the street or open a magazine or newspaper, you see advertising in all of these places. Every year enormous sums of money are spent on advertising, and for one reason only: it works. How does it work, or what does it work on?

Does it work only on the people who see it, or does it have a broader effect? Experiments have shown that once a small number of rats have learned how to navigate a maze, it becomes easier for any succeeding rats to find their way. Speculation is that rats have a form of collective consciousness, and the actions of a relatively small number of individual rats can, so to speak, blaze a trail in the collective consciousness that makes it easier for others to learn a task. It has been shown that it is far easier for the average physics student today to understand the theory of relativity than it was 80 years ago. It seems that physics students, like rats, have a collective consciousness (no other comparison intended or implied).

What does advertising work on? It might indeed work on this collective consciousness so that once a critical mass of people have started buying one brand of toothpaste over another, it becomes easier to persuade others to buy it. This is why companies spend a lot of money on an initial advertising blitz and then go to a lower level that still gives them a growth in sales. Likewise, political opinions can sometimes shift very quickly once a critical mass is reached. Why is it that after years of smaller protests, suddenly tens of thousands of people flood the streets and a dictatorial regime is overthrown almost overnight? Why is it that after centuries of slavery being an accepted norm, it suddenly became obvious to most people in Western nations that it was no longer acceptable?

There does seem to be a collective consciousness, and it is possible to bring about changes in society by affecting the collective mind. In the beginning, this will seem like an uphill climb, but at some point a critical mass is reached. Suddenly, the collective consciousness – and public opinion – shifts almost instantly. By educating yourself and voicing your opinion, you can indeed make a contribution that will pull the collective consciousness in a certain direction. If enough other people do the same, a critical mass will eventually be reached and public opinion can shift very quickly.

Let us look at what science has to say about the existence of a collective mind. Before we can fully understand the collective mind, it is necessary to consider that science has pointed toward the need for a new world view, a view that is a quantum leap beyond our existing mental box.

A relatively new world view

What does the theory of relativity – and its basic formula, $E=mc^2$ – actually tell us? Before Einstein, scientists had a very specific view of the world, and we might call it a dualistic view. They believed the world was made of two fundamentally different substances or elements, namely matter and energy. Matter was made of microscopic particles that were like miniature billiard balls, having no internal parts and therefore being indivisible. Energy was made of waves that were constantly fluctuating and could be divided or changed almost indefinitely. Physicists were absolutely convinced that energy and matter were so fundamentally different that one could not possibly be converted into the other.

In order to understand this world view, take a glass of water and pour some salt into it. You can see the salt particles at the bottom of the glass, but if you stir the water, the salt crystals disappear and you see only water. This does not mean that salt has now been turned into water. It means that a chemical reaction has taken place whereby the microscopic salt molecules have mixed with the water molecules so the salt crystals are no longer visible—they have been dissolved by the water. The salt crystals that were visible have been broken up into smaller parts that are invisible. The molecules of the salt are mixed in with the molecules of the water so your eyes see only water.

If you pour the water into a pot and boil it, the water will evaporate and the salt crystals will reappear at the bottom of the pot. Water and salt can mix, but one cannot be converted into the other. If you had claimed that salt could be turned into water, any pre-einsteinian scientist would have laughed you to scorn and compared you to the medieval alchemists who thought they could turn lead into gold. After Einstein, there is no longer any basis for that scorn.

What Einstein's simple formula proves is that the dualistic world view is not correct. Matter and energy are not fundamentally different elements. By putting energy (E) on one side of the equal sign and mass or matter (m) on the other side, Einstein proved that matter can indeed be converted into energy and vice versa. The deeper understanding that emerges from Einstein's work is that everything is created from energy.

It is not incorrect to say that matter does not exist. Matter is a form of energy that no longer freely moves like a wave but has been (temporarily) captured into a stationary form of vibration, what is called an energy field.

What we call matter is a mental construct based on our sensory perception. Our senses cannot detect the extremely fast vibrations in the energy field of a rock, and thus we detect it as a solid substance. Compare this to looking at an airplane propeller that spins so fast that your eyes cannot see the propeller blades but see a "solid" disc. A rock is simply an energy field that is constantly vibrating, and so is your body and the entire earth body. What we see as matter is truly a sea of energy.

The problem with Einstein's theory is precisely that it contradicts our sensory experience, and that is why even most scientists to this day resist the philosophical implications of the theory. These implications demand that we question the world view that is based on our senses, a world view we have had for thousands of years without truly questioning it. This sensory-based, dualistic world view is dead—and this has profound implications for developing a new approach to evil.

Locality is dead, long live non-locality

The essential characteristic of the sensory-based world view is a concept that in physics is called "locality." This idea says that things can be separate, that one "thing" can have an existence as being separated from other things or even from a larger whole. As an example, consider a demonstration that you probably saw in school. You take a large number of iron filings and spread them on a sheet of cardboard. The filings are distributed randomly, and if you look closer, you can see that the individual filings are resting on the cardboard with some distance between them. Your eyes see no connection between the filings, and this gives the impression that they exist independently of each other. Each filing is a separate unit.

The existence of such separate, independent units is integral to the sensory-based world view that has ruled our Western civilization unchallenged for thousands of years. It is integral to our way of thinking about ourselves and our relationship with each other. It is a major factor (one might say *the* major factor) in the creation of evil. The fact that this world view has now been rendered obsolete by science is monumental—but let's not get ahead of ourselves.

Back to the iron filings on the cardboard. Imagine that someone places a bar magnet underneath the sheet of cardboard. The supposedly separate and independent iron filings organize themselves into a distinct pattern of elliptical lines. To our senses this makes absolutely no sense because we can see nothing that directly acted upon the individual filings. We can explain this only by going beyond our senses. The explanation we were all given in school is that a magnet creates an invisible field around itself. The iron filings are magnetic, meaning they are affected by the field and pulled into the pattern we see on the cardboard. Although this explanation goes beyond what our senses can detect, it is still affected by the sensory-based view of the world.

The explanation still looks at each iron filing as an independent unit. It exists as a separate unit and it will not move unless an external, independent force acts upon it—in this case the magnet. Your senses seem to support this view, as you can see that an iron filing does not move as long as there is no magnet that is close enough to the cardboard. It seems reasonable that the iron filing is a separate unit and so is the magnet. The problem here is that this is not the case, which has been proven by a branch of physics that was developed based on

Einstein's findings. It is called quantum mechanics, and it has definitively killed locality.

Quantum physics was developed in order to study subatomic particles, the smaller building blocks that make up the atom. Many of us were taught the so-called planetary model of the atom where the core of the atom is made up of protons and neutrons with a number of electrons orbiting around it, like planets around the sun. The problem with this model is that it is sensory-based so it illustrates each subatomic particle as a distinct dot. This gives the impression that a subatomic particle is an isolated unit that can be ripped out of an atom and studied independently. Quantum physics has proven that this is not the case.

The first serious challenge to the sensory-based world view came in the 1930s when quantum physicists came up with something called the double-slit experiment. I am not going to go into detail here because the experiment has been described in dozens of popular books on quantum physics. The mind-boggling discovery made by this experiment is that what scientists had considered a microscopic billiard ball is something else entirely. Let us talk about a subatomic "entity" instead of a "particle."

If the double-slit experiment is conducted in a certain way, the subatomic entity behaves like one would expect from a traditional particle—a single unit traveling through an empty space and not affected by any external forces. If the experiment is conducted in a different way, the subatomic entity behaves as one would expect from a wave that is extended through space and propagating through a medium.

At first, this experiment was shocking to physicists, and it is still baffling to many of them today, but quantum physicists have come up with even more mind-boggling experiments. It turns out that physicists can create a pair of subatomic entities that are linked through a particular characteristic, such as spin. You can then separate the entities by a great distance, yet if you change the spin of one entity, you will instantly – *instantly* – see a change in the spin of the other entity.

According to classical physics, this is nothing short of impossible. In classical physics nothing is instantaneous. If two classical particles are separated in space, they are separate, isolated units; there is no connecting link between them. If there is a change in one particle, then the only way this can generate a change in the other particle is if some kind of signal is sent from one particle to the other. Any signal must – according to Einstein – travel at or below the speed of light. If there is distance, no signal can cross that distance instantaneously. The greater the distance, the greater the time before the one particle will know what the other is doing.

Such experiments are highly disturbing to people who hold on to the classical, sensory-based view of the world. These experiments have been conducted many times and they have been scrutinized very carefully by people who would love to prove them wrong. The experiments have passed all tests, and there is only one logical conclusion. Despite what our sensory-based world view has been telling us for thousands of years, we do not live in a localized universe. A philosopher once said that: "No man is an island." It turns out that no *thing* is an island. There is no such thing as a distinct unit that has an isolated existence. Locality is an idea in the mind, not an actual reality.

Our universe is *not* made up of a large number of separate units that just happen to be floating around in the same space but are not connected unless they bump into each other or exchange some kind of force. Instead, our universe is one large interconnected whole in which nothing is independent of the whole.

The basis for human evil is the very concept of locality, namely that we human beings are separate, independent units that just happen to live on the same planet. This gives rise to a very specific belief, namely that because you and I are separate persons, I can harm you without affecting myself. Say you have something I want. If I am stronger than you and if there is no one stronger than me, such as the police and judicial system, then I can take what you have. I have enriched myself, and if you and I really are separate units, the harm I have done to you has not in any way affected myself.

The concept of locality is the basis for most conflicts and violence. It is also the basis for primitive societies that were based on the "law of the jungle," namely that might is right. This explains why it is so essential to question locality. If we ever are to develop a new approach to human evil, how can we possibly do so without looking beyond locality? Trying to do so would be attempting to solve a problem with the very same consciousness that created the problem.

Our civilized societies have already started to move beyond locality. The extreme outcome of locality is the law of the jungle. All civilized nations have risen above this and see it as primitive. Instead, we have replaced it with the concept of rights, and we have created ways to directly curb the desire to harm others through various forms of punishment. The hidden message is that you cannot harm others without harming yourself.

What if there was an even deeper connection between people, a connection that would make it clear that when you harm others, you do actually harm yourself? Such a connection has been suggested by most religions. They all contain some variant of a concept that we in the West know from Jesus' statement: "Do unto others as you want them to do unto you." This statement is a clear challenge to locality because it suggests a deeper connection between us whereby what I do to you will directly reflect back upon myself.

Is it possible that the most sophisticated branch of modern science is now beginning to converge with ancient mystical traditions and that both are pointing to the need to transcend the illusion of locality? Is it possible that the next logical step for the human race is to take a quantum leap beyond locality and develop a higher approach to all aspects of life, including human conflict and the problem of evil? Let us take a closer look at locality and see where it comes from.

6 | WANTED: A NON-LOCAL WORLD VIEW

Locality is highly tied to the senses, which do tell us that we live in a world with separate and distinct forms. Locality is not entirely produced by the senses but also by a specific element in the human psyche. Locality is a very persuasive concept because we can all see many distinct and separate forms around us. Locality is possibly the most subtle and difficult to overcome illusion faced by human beings. This explains why we have not yet truly risen above it and why we still experience the evil that is the consequence of locality.

Why is locality such a persuasive illusion? One answer is that it is difficult for us to question our direct perception. Why should we question the accuracy of what we can see with our own eyes? The obvious reason is that our physical senses have certain limitations. For one thing, they have a limited range. Our eyes can detect light that vibrates within a certain spectrum of frequencies but cannot detect light of higher or lower frequencies. We also know that our eyes can be fooled. We have all seen examples of optical illusions, such as two lines that are the same length. Because one line has arrows at each end pointing inward and the other line has arrows pointing outward, they appear to be of different length. We have all seen the old drawing that at one moment looks like a beautiful young girl and at the next moment looks like an old lady.

The history of science has been a process of helping us look beyond our senses. Cells, molecules, atoms and subatomic particles are all too small to be seen with the naked eye, yet we accept that they exist. By recognizing their existence, we have been able to expand our knowledge and develop many forms of technology that would not be possible with visible objects.

Locality is not only a question of what our senses can actually detect—it is also a question of how our minds interpret what we see. Let us revisit the experiment of the iron filings on the cardboard. Your eyes tell you that each iron filing is a separate unit that is not connected to the other filings (unless they directly touch each other), but is this really true? The link that connects all of the iron filings on the cardboard is – of course – the cardboard. All of the filings touch it, and through that contact they are also connected to each other. If you tilt the cardboard, the filings all start sliding. This little example shows us something very important about how our senses – and a part of our minds – work.

Consider that you are looking at a blank sheet of paper. Your eyes can't find anything to focus on because there is no contrast, there is nothing that stands out. Now draw one black dot on the paper and your eyes are instantly attracted to it. Draw more dots, and sooner or later your eyes will see only the dots and forget about the paper—as you have been doing while reading this book. The letters you read are compilations of black dots, and you have no doubt been focusing on the dots while paying little attention to the white background behind them. Yet could the letters exist without the background? Our senses and part of our minds are designed to detect contrast and differences. The parts of our brains that deal with sensory input are wired to "look" for distinct forms. Put a number of dots on a sheet of paper, and your brain is going to start looking for patterns that can form letters, that can form words, to which your mind can attach some form of meaning.

I am not saying there is anything wrong with this. It is a perfectly natural mechanism based on the need to survive in the physical world. We need a way to quickly identify forms that can pose a danger or identify forms that mean food. Naturally, our senses are designed for this purpose. While there is nothing inherently wrong with it, this sensory-based form of thinking does have certain limitations.

Our tendency to focus on contrast makes us see the iron filings and overlook the cardboard, makes us see the letters and overlook the background. If we only consider the world from our sensory-based perspective, we will tend to see it as made up of distinct forms and we will overlook any connecting link.

A distinct form is distinct because it is different from other forms, as the dots on a piece of paper stand out from the non-distinct paper. A link that connects all forms must by its nature be non-distinct, as the white paper itself. Our senses and the sensory-based aspect of the mind are likely to overlook the non-distinct connecting link. We simply *won't* see it—not because we *can't* see it but because we are so focused on what makes us different that we overlook what unites us.

It is the impression that we are separate beings that makes it possible for us to commit evil acts towards other people. If we are to transcend evil, we have to find a connecting link between us. That link will never be found through sensory-based perception but only by using the mind's ability to think and imagine beyond what we detect with our senses. In order to move toward a new approach to human evil, we need to go beyond a sensory-based world view and look for something that serves as a connecting link between us, and potentially between all forms. Instead of focusing on what separates us, let us look for something that connects us.

The missing link

Quantum physicists have conducted experiments which show that even if two subatomic entities are separated by a great distance, a change in one entity leads to an instantaneous change in the other entity. This cannot be explained by saying that a signal was sent from one particle to the other because such a signal cannot travel faster than the speed of light and thus cannot account for an instantaneous change.

The explanation can be found by applying a universal principle that is behind all human progress: If an observed phenomenon cannot be explained by our present world view, it is time to question that world view. We can either continue to wring our hands in amazement, or we can start questioning the sensory-based world view. After all, it is precisely this view that has given rise to the belief that we live in a world made up of separate "things."

Science has proven that two entities, although separated by "empty" space, are not separate. There must be a hidden connection between them; we simply have not yet discovered it. We can now start looking for such a connection.

Our first clue comes from relativity. Einstein's formula truly says that there is no such "thing" as matter. Matter is a mental construct, a product of the sensory-based world view. In reality, every "thing" is made from vibrating energy. Our senses are simply designed to detect energies within a certain frequency spectrum. Because our physical bodies are made from energy that vibrates within the same spectrum, matter seems solid to our physical senses. Even our bodies fool our senses. We think they are solid, but in reality, they are made of smaller units, called cells. The cells are made from even smaller units, called molecules—that are made from atoms, which are made from subatomic particles. As the planetary model of the atom shows, an atom is made up mostly of empty space, which means even our bodies are mostly empty space. There truly is nothing "solid" in the universe.

Let us now go to a deeper level than visible forms. As the double-slit experiment proves, the most basic level of matter seems to have a dual nature. A subatomic entity can behave as both a particle and a wave. At the level of subatomic entities, we have reached the border between matter and energy. Subatomic entities are normally pure energy, but under certain conditions they take on the appearance of solid matter particles, the particles that make up every "thing" in the material universe. The conclusion is clear: The connecting link between everything cannot be found at the level of matter—it is not some kind of solid substance. It must be found at the underlying level of pure energy, or perhaps even at a deeper level.

If you ask a scientist what energy is, you will either get a blank stare or an explanation about waves propagating through a medium. The most obvious example is waves on the ocean or in a bathtub. Saying that everything is made up of energy does raise a problem, namely: "What is vibrating, what is the medium through which the waves are propagating?" Sound is normally energy waves propagating through the medium of the air.

Since childhood, we have been told that the universe is vast and that stars are so far away that it takes a light wave millions of years to reach earth. We have also been told that if we travel outside earth's atmosphere, we go into empty space. The term "empty space" will make the sensory-based mind think there is nothing there. Yet if space truly is empty, then what is the medium through which light waves from a star propagate to reach us? Waves are vibrations of a medium. If there is no medium, there can be no waves—unless our understanding of waves is incomplete.

A couple of hundred years ago, physicists had an easy answer. Back then, they believed empty space was not empty but was filled with an invisible substance, called the "ether." Unfortunately, their conception of the ether was that it had physical properties, and this made a couple of physicists decide that it should be possible to measure an "ether wind" generated as the earth moves through space. They set up an experiment and failed to detect the ether wind, which made most physicists conclude that the ether does not exist. This is a good example of the persuasiveness of the sensory-based world view. No scientist raised the question of whether the instruments were simply too crude to detect the ether wind.

In recent years, other scientists have used far better instruments and have in fact detected something similar to an ether wind. Other scientists have pointed to an invisible substance through other routes, including quantum physics. For example, it has been observed that a subatomic particle can appear our of "nowhere," divide itself into several other particles that travel a short distance and then collide with each other only to disappear. Where did these particles come from in the first place? Scientists talk about a quantum field that is a level of vibration or energy so fine that it cannot be detected by current scientific instruments. It is nevertheless still very real and is, in fact, the very foundation for everything we *can* detect.

Physicists have clearly started to point beyond what science has traditionally called the material universe. A growing number of experiments and theories point to the existence of something beyond our current powers of observation. This something is not only real, but it is also the womb out of which both matter and energy are born. Scientists are on the verge of discovering a connecting link that unifies everything that exists in the visible universe.

What could possibly be non-local?

Let us again go back to the quantum experiment where two particles are separated by a great distance and where a change to the spin of one particle leads to an instantaneous change in the spin of the other particle. Even energy waves cannot explain this, for they cannot move faster than the speed of light. So far, scientists have been baffled by this because they are operating with the basic assumption – generated by Einstein – that nothing can move faster than the speed of light.

What if our entire problem here is that we are still looking at the world through the filter of the sensory-based mind? This mind firmly believes in locality so it must seek to explain everything as a localized phenomenon. If there is a link between two separated entities, some form of signal must be exchanged.

What if we recognized that science has – definitively – pointed beyond locality, and thus we need to free our minds from the filter of locality? As one example, take the wave-particle duality. When a subatomic entity behaves like a particle, it clearly has locality—it exists as a distinct particle that can be found in a specific location in space. When the subatomic entity behaves like a wave, it is not localized in one point but extends throughout space (yet still being localized in the sense that it moves through space). According to a sensory-based view, the same entity cannot be both a wave or a particle—it must be one or the other, but there is an obvious alternative. What if we simply recognized that there are no waves or particles? "Wave" and "particle" are not actual entities but are mental constructs that we have imposed upon reality. Because both waves and particles are localized phenomena, they are born from a sensory-based world view. By insisting that a subatomic entity must be either a wave or a particle, we are trying to force the universe to fit into our current mental box. Numerous scientific experiments have proven that the universe stubbornly refuses to fit itself into our box, meaning that the box is the problem, not the universe. A subatomic entity is neither a wave nor a particle, but as long as we insist that it must be one or the other we will not be able to "see" it for what it really is. Instead of seeing the subatomic entity as it is, we are constantly trying to project a mental image onto it—an image crafted from our sensory-based world view.

We are frantically trying to validate our localized world view by making everything in the universe appear as localized phenomena. Experiments consistently point to the fact that the universe is not localized. Whatever a subatomic entity really is, it is not a localized "thing," meaning we need to start looking for something non-local.

Let us again look at the two quantum particles. They are separated by a great distance in space and no signals – physical particles or energy waves – are sent between them. How do we explain an instantaneous connection? It must be a non-local connection. The connection must be in the form of a phenomenon that is not dependent upon locality—meaning time and space. Before you start thinking Star Trek and warp speed, let me assure you that this phenomenon is something you deal with every day—you simply don't notice it, as you don't see the white background behind the letters in this book. Imagine a thought experiment. We are at the Great Wall of China.

At each end is one of our friends, equipped with a flashlight. Each person has been told to turn the light on or off randomly. Since our two friends cannot see each other, there is no connection between them—there are no signals passing from one to the other.

You are positioned so that you can see both persons at the same time. When one person turns on her flashlight, she doesn't know whether the other person has his light on or off. Yet *you* know because you see both of them at the same time. There is no connection between the two in terms of signals sent from one to the other, yet there is a connection. That connection is your mind. You know the status of each light without any signals being sent between the two people. Beyond a physical connection could be a connection in consciousness.

Science and the mind

I earlier said that scientific materialism is a political system developed by an aspiring power elite for the purpose of usurping the position of the religious power elite. The proof is that the scientific establishment has completely ignored one of the most challenging findings of quantum physics. Quantum mechanics is both the most controversial and the most successful scientific theory of all time. Its predictions have been scrutinized more than any other theory, but they have never been proven wrong. The most important conclusion coming from this theory has been completely ignored by the scientific establishment, and the reason is that this discovery conclusively proves the fallacy of scientific materialism.

The most challenging discovery of quantum physics was made as far back as the 1930s, and it started with the double-slit experiment. Physicists realized that when they conducted the double-slit experiment in a way designed to detect particles, the subatomic entities would obediently behave like particles. When conducted it a different way, the same subatomic entities would obediently behave like waves. The outcome of the experiment was directly dependent upon the intent, the choices, made by the physicist. The result of the experiment could not be separated from the consciousness of the scientist!

This discovery threatens the very foundation of materialism—which is why it has been ignored. Materialistic science was developed as a challenge to religion. Materialists took advantage of the fact that at the level of the senses, it seems like we can conduct experiments that give the same outcome regardless of the beliefs of the scientists. If you take a Muslim, a Jew and a Christian to the top of a building and have them each drop a lead weight, they will all fall to the ground and they will fall with the same speed. The very foundation for materialistic science is the belief that there exists phenomena that are independent of our consciousness. This is what allowed materialists to claim that religious doctrines and beliefs are the result of superstition – a subjective phenomenon produced by the mind – whereas scientific results are objective, meaning not affected by the human mind.

For almost two centuries, this claim to objectivity has been the cornerstone of materialism, and to a large degree of science itself. It is based on a localized view of the world, namely a view that creates an inseparable barrier between the scientist and the phenomenon he or she is observing. Scientists believe that if there is no physical connection, they can observe a phenomenon without having their minds affect the outcome of the observation. They talk about scientists being *objective* observers—as opposed to religious people (even all non-scientists) who are *subjective* observers of life. Through the double-slit experiment physicists discovered that the consciousness of the scientist is *not* separated from the subatomic entity. A subatomic entity will respond to the consciousness of the scientist, meaning that the outcome of any experiment is a product of what is called the "entire measurement situation." The measurement situation consists of three elements, namely the subatomic entity, the instrument used to measure it (such as a particle accelerator) and the consciousness of the physicist.

The logical conclusion is that at the level of subatomic entities, there is no such thing as an objective or neutral observer. A physicist is not observing an entity that exists independently of consciousness. The subatomic entity doesn't actually exist before the observation is made. A physicist is co-creating the entity he is observing by making the observation.

This conclusion – which has been tested over an over again – was in itself highly disturbing to all materialists, and that is why it has been largely ignored by the mainstream scientific establishment. Things become even more radical when we take the observations of quantum mechanics a logical step further.

In order to avoid pulling the rug from under materialism, some scientists have argued that the findings of quantum physics are relevant only in the subatomic world and do not apply to the so-called macroscopic world, meaning the world we see with our senses. The undeniable fact is that everything in the macroscopic world is made from subatomic entities so how can we separate the two? We can do so only when we see through the filter of the sensory-based world view, which can indeed create divisions and separation.

The entire history of science has challenged this localized world view. Saying that what is true in the subatomic world has no relevance in the macroscopic world goes against the entire history of science—and logic.

Quantum physics has decisively killed locality by proving that there is a connecting link between everything, from the microscopic to the macroscopic. That link is not some objective entity "out there," but it is a link of consciousness. Quantum physics has proven conclusively and undeniably that at the most fundamental level of the material world, consciousness is present.

How can we explain that a subatomic entity can respond to the consciousness of a scientist? You either have to accept mind over matter or you have to draw the conclusion that a subatomic entity either is made of consciousness or is directed by some form of consciousness. Either way, you kill materialism and the localized world view upon which it is based.

Why is this so significant in terms of developing a new approach to human evil? We started out by saying that evil is based on locality, namely the illusion that we are separate entities, and thus I can harm you without hurting myself. Without this sense of separation – if we see ourselves as connected – no evil is possible. If we are to overcome evil, we have to find a connecting link between all of us. We now see that the existence of such a link has been proven by science, and the link is indeed consciousness.

This is monumental because if we truly want to understand the cause of evil, we need to stop looking outside ourselves. We tend to explain conflict between groups of people in terms of political, economic or sociological factors. We now see that although these factors may affect human behavior, they cannot explain the real cause of evil. In order to find that cause, we have to start looking inside ourselves, at the human psyche, the human mind. The real cause of evil must be found in consciousness.

According to science, locality is an illusion. Everything in the world is connected, and the connection is consciousness. Locality is a very persuasive illusion that springs from our sensory-based perception of the world. Where is the sensory-based, localized world view created? In our consciousness, of course. We can now make a very simple, yet very constructive, conclusion. There must be a factor in the human mind that not only creates the illusion of locality but also makes it seem so believable that for the greater part of human history most people have never questioned it.

The beauty of this conclusion is that if one aspect of the mind has created the illusion of separation and locality, then there might be another aspect of the mind that can help us see beyond it. Indeed, certain spiritual teachers might already have shown us various ways to escape the illusion of locality. It seems our next step is to look for the mechanism that creates the illusion of locality and makes it so believable.

7 | THE ORIGIN OF THE ILLUSION OF LOCALITY

Let me summarize what we have considered so far:

- One of the major causes, if not *the* major cause, of human evil is the illusion of locality, the sense that we are separate beings and thus I can hurt you without harming myself.

- The illusion of locality is tied to our senses and how we look at the world through our senses.

- It is difficult to question what we "see" through our senses.

- We have risen from a more primitive stage to modern civilization because we have asked questions outside our current mental box, including our sensory-based mental box.

- Science has empowered us to discover a level of reality that is beyond the reach of the senses.

How is it possible that we – meaning humankind as a whole – have not truly questioned and transcended the illusion of locality? How come this illusion has persisted for so long? Part of the explanation is a power elite that wants to set itself above the general population. The mindset of such a power elite is clearly based on the illusion of locality. It is this illusion that makes it possible to divide humankind into separate groups and then impose a value judgment upon the groups, one being superior and others being inferior. We have considered the following about a power elite:

- Any historical period has had one or more power elite groups vying for ultimate control.

- Such control can only be attained by controlling the thinking of the general population so that the people will not use their numerical superiority against the elite.

- A power elite group attempted to use science in order to control people's thinking and get them to accept a self-image that is ultimately dis-empowering and thus allows the power elite that generated it to stay in a superior position.

- Science is truly an open-ended process and this process has now effectively dis-proven the materialistic world view.

This has been ignored or suppressed by the dominant power elite, yet the real question is why such a large part of the population still believes in the materialistic world view? This world view is not really enforced with any military power so why haven't the people challenged it openly or simply stopped believing it? Could it be that many people do not want to give up this world view, even if it is out of touch with reality?

Is it possible that there is a mechanism that makes us want to believe in an illusion, even when it has been proven to be an illusion? Is it possible there is a mechanism that won't allow us to embrace a new world view, a view based on reality? Is it possible that this mechanism predisposes us to uphold status quo by refusing to seriously question our mental box?

In order to gain a wider perspective on this, let us go even further back in history. The materialistic world view was not developed to set our minds free. It was developed to challenge the position of the religious power elite. As such it had to challenge the world view presented by religion, specifically the medieval Catholic Church. Where did this world view come from? Most people would say that it is based on the teachings of Jesus, but is that really true?

The world view presented by the medieval Catholic Church is a text-book example of a localized view. The church claimed to be the only true church of Jesus Christ and that Jesus was the only doorway to heaven. This divides humanity into two distinct groups, Catholics and non-Catholics. The Catholics will – if they obey the church – be saved whereas the others will not. This world view creates an irreconcilable conflict between Catholics and other people, which is clearly demonstrated by such undeniable historical events as the burning of books, the Crusades, the massacre of the Cathars, the witch hunts, the Inquisition and the suppression of scientists.

Was Jesus a teacher of locality or non-locality? Did Jesus present a localized or a non-localized world view? Jesus' own words contain many statements that clearly point beyond locality. For example, the Jews of Jesus' time had a localized view, seeing themselves as God's chosen people and all others as belonging to a lower class of unclean people. Jesus went out of his way to have contact with Samaritans, lepers, sinners and tax collectors. He even showed that such people could be allowed entry into the kingdom of God, thereby hinting that this kingdom is not based on a localized world view. The kingdom of God in non-local, and only the kingdoms of men are local.

Jesus made numerous statements that point beyond locality. For example, Jesus declared non-locality in a vertical way by saying: "I and my father are one," thus declaring himself one with something beyond what the senses can see. He also declared non-locality in a horizontal way by saying: "Inasmuch as ye have done it unto the least of these my brethren, ye have done it unto me," thus declaring his essential oneness with all people—and thereby indirectly declaring the oneness of all people.

When I learned that the religion that claims to represent Christ had committed the above mentioned atrocities, I was absolutely stunned. Here we have a religion that claims to represent Christ—the Christ who told us not to resist evil. If a person slaps us on one cheek, we should not hit back but turn the other cheek. At the same time, this religion obviously isn't following the commands of the one they claim to be representing. Even as a child it was obvious to me that there is a glaring discrepancy between the teachings of Christ and the behavior of Christians. How do we explain this?

What if Jesus actually came to help us rise above the localized world view? He came to offer us a non-local view that could empower us to go beyond the very mindset that is the cause of human evil. If we had truly accepted and incorporated Jesus' original, non-local teachings, we might have avoided many of the conflicts we have seen over the past 2,000 years, especially the ones created by Christianity itself.

How do we explain that a non-local spiritual teaching was turned into a religious organization that clearly promotes and lives by a localized world view? We can look at the historical record and see that for three centuries, the Christian movement was not very clearly defined. It had many different factions, some of which did actually teach non-locality. It was the Roman emperor Constantine I who turned Christianity into a religion. After Christianity became the official state religion of the Roman empire, it went through a major transformation that effectively suppressed all elements of non-locality. This turned the Catholic Church into a very effective mind control machine that managed to control people's thinking for over a thousand years.

We can't quite explain this by the existence of a power elite because we also have to explain why the majority followed the elite. The obvious explanation is that the majority of the population gained what they considered an advantage from accepting the localized world view of the elite. What might that advantage be?

Medieval people lived under appalling conditions with poverty, disease, war and terrible living conditions. If we go into the mindset of medieval people, they did not see themselves as we see them. They saw themselves as belonging to the most sophisticated civilization ever (actually, on that point they are were much like us) and they accepted most of their living conditions as simply unavoidable (again, much like us).

The real difference is that medieval people were not all that concerned about the conditions on earth. They were focused on what they would gain in the life they believed was coming after earth. Medieval Christians believed they would be granted a wonderful afterlife in a heavenly world whereas all non-Christians would burn forever in a fiery hell. Enduring a few hardships on earth – including submitting to a power elite – was a small price to pay for an eternity in paradise.

Medieval people were programmed to believe this because it allowed the power elite to control them. The underlying message was that if the people allowed the elite to rule them here on earth, God would reward them in heaven. This gave the earth to the elite and prevented the people from challenging the power and privilege of their rulers. Nevertheless, there must have been a reason why the people accepted this world view—it must have offered them an advantage. The advantage was that the people did not have to take responsibility for their lives. They did not have to think for themselves and make their own decisions; they did not have to take command over their own destinies. They could believe what they were told to believe, and then they were guaranteed a reward in heaven. We can now take two distinct roads forward.

We can identify the power elite as the promoters of the localized world view and thus appoint them as the cause of all of humanity's problems. We can turn the power elite into a scapegoat, thinking that if only we get rid of the elite, we will solve all of our problems. We can have another French revolution, in which we identify the members of the power elite and decapitate them. Let's get on the barricades and bring out Madame la Guillotine!

Would this approach actually help to decrease human evil, or would it perpetuate the very mindset that is the underlying cause of evil? This is the mindset of locality where we divide humankind into at least two groups, namely "us" versus "them." Then we say that "us" are always right and "them" are always wrong so we need to get rid of "them."

Obviously, this approach will do nothing to reduce evil. We need to find a different approach and it must be non-local. It cannot identify the problem as being "out there," saying that it is found only in other people. Instead, we must be willing to look "in here" and recognize that the real cause of conflict is a mechanism in the human psyche—the human psyche that all of us share.

I propose a new approach to identifying the cause of evil. Instead of looking for it outside ourselves, we must look for an element in the human psyche that makes us prone to see the world through the filter of locality. This element sees only locality and it even seeks to prevent us from seeing beyond this illusion—seeing the underlying reality of non-locality. Our next step will be to look for this psychological mechanism or element.

Introducing the ego

The element in the human psyche that believes in locality or seeks to make us believe in locality is easy to identify, as it has been a subject of study for psychologists, self-help experts and spiritual teachers for some time. It is commonly called "the ego." As scientists find it difficult to define what energy is, there is no widespread consensus about how to define the ego. The word itself comes from Greek and means the "I" or the self. In its broadest definition, the ego is your sense of self as an individual.

Sigmund Freud used the word differently, in the sense had he divided the psyche into three "layers." The lowest is the "id" which is made up of instinctual drives, such as the survival instinct. In the middle is what Freud called the ego, and he saw it as the conscious mind that makes practical, every-day decisions. On top of that is the super-ego which is the seat of moral and ethical concerns. According to Freud's definition, the causes of evil is more likely found in the id than in the ego.

Beginning with Carl Jung, a number of psychologists and self-help experts have developed a different way to use the concept of the ego. The ego has come to be seen as an element in the psyche that makes us self-centered, selfish and egotistical. According to this use of the word, the ego is the very cause of all human evil. It is the ego that makes us believe we are separate, independent beings and that if I harm you, I won't hurt myself.

It is this latter use of the word ego that I will take as our starting point for further exploration. The reason is that the concept is useful in several ways when it comes to explaining human evil:

- The concept of the ego states that there is an element in the human psyche that makes us prone to commit evil acts and that prevents us from rising above evil.

- This is an element that all of us have so we cannot point the finger at anyone else and project the cause as being "out there." The cause is in the psyche so we must all be willing to look at the beam – the ego – in our own eye.

- The ego is a distinct element of the psyche. This makes it easier to study the ego and understand how it affects our behavior. Even if we have no clear or unanimous definition of ego, we do have a good understanding of how it works. We can easily describe the most obvious effects of the ego, such as selfishness, fear, anger, blame etc.

• The ego is an element in the psyche, but it is not the whole of the psyche. We have the possibility of isolating the ego and then seeing that we are more than the ego.

The latter point is especially important for a discussion about evil. If it is the human psyche itself, our very nature, that makes us prone to evil, then what hope do we have of transcending evil? Why waste time writing a book if we can't change ourselves anyway? If the cause of evil is an identifiable element of the psyche, but not the whole of the psyche or the basic nature of the psyche, then we have the hope of being able to separate some aspect of the psyche from the ego and thus transcend the ego and its effects.

Why I will not define the ego—yet

If the cause of human evil is the ego, why not start by defining the ego? In order to explain this, I would like to point to a concept that all of us are familiar with, but we are so familiar with it that we hardly notice it. In this world, everything is a matter of finding a balance between two extremes. Everything has advantages and disadvantages, and we need to consider both in order to choose the best possible approach.

In the Western world we tend to have a very practical and action-oriented approach to life. The advantage of this approach is that we have made great technological and organizational progress. We have a wonderful modern civilization and a high material standard of living. The disadvantage is that we tend to ignore the more subtle aspects of life, such as quality of life.

Despite our progress, more and more people are beginning to realize that taking care of people's material needs will not automatically make them happy. Because we are reluctant to question our basic approach to life, we can't seem to find an approach that will produce happiness. You might have heard the saying that if the only tool you have is a hammer, every problem becomes a nail, and it sums up our experience as a civilization. We are still caught up in thinking that if our present level of material abundance hasn't made us happy, then it must be because we need even more material wealth—and *then* we will be happy.

How does this relate to defining the ego? Our Western mindset is very action-oriented. When we face a problem, we want to identify and isolate a single, clearly-defined cause of the problem and then we want to focus all of our efforts on destroying that cause. We are absolutely sure that if we isolate and destroy the cause of a problem, then the problem will go away. If we identify the cause of evil as the ego, we want to launch a search-and-destroy mission against the ego.

This simply isn't going to work. The full answer will not become clear until we gain a deeper understanding of the ego, as we will do in coming chapters. The short answer can be found in Albert Einstein's saying: "You can't solve a problem with the same state of consciousness that created the problem."

The human ego presents a unique challenge to us. You will not overcome the ego by seeking to deal with it from the same state of consciousness, the same mindset, created by the ego. Trying to do this will only reinforce the ego and thus it will not reduce but add to the evil in the world. In order to overcome the ego, we need to get out of the mental box created by the ego. We need to start thinking in a way that is not colored by the ego, a way that outsmarts or transcends the ego.

The problem is that the ego has a very subtle effect on our thinking or the way we look at life. Imagine that it is a beautiful spring day where the birds are singing and the sun is smiling from a deep, blue sky. You decide to take a walk, and at first you are truly enjoying the quiet morning. Then you become aware of an annoying noise, and as you walk closer, you see two people arguing on the sidewalk. They are yelling at the top of their voices and they seem so angry that it is just a matter of time before they start fighting. As you come closer, you can begin to hear what they are saying, and to your amazement, you overhear the following conversation:

Person One: "You are completely blind, you fool, everyone can tell that the sky is green. This isn't a subject for debate, it is just a matter of seeing reality!"

Person Two: "Only a complete moron can deny the obvious. Anyone who is not blind can see the sky is purple! Don't give me all that stuff about your view being superior; this is just a matter of seeing reality!"

At first you are completely baffled by this. The two people sound so sure that you cast a quick glance at the sky, just to make sure that it really is blue. You think: "What is going on here?" Then you notice that one person is wearing yellow glasses and the other is wearing red glasses. You remember your basic physics lesson that if you look through a colored lens, certain colors will be changed. A yellow lens will turn blue into green whereas a red lens will turn blue into purple. You now have an "Aha-moment" and realize that the entire cause of the two people's argument is that none of them are realizing that they are wearing colored glasses.

As the argument is getting more and more angry, you realize you have to do something, but what exactly is the best approach here? Would it be smart to jump into the fray and start arguing that both persons are wrong and that none of them are seeing reality because the sky really is blue? Imagine how the two persons might react if you did that. They are likely to reject your arguments, each of them saying: "I am seeing it with my own eyes!" In a sense they are right—they really are seeing the sky as a particular color. You simply can't argue with that, so what can you do? After thinking about it for a few seconds, you spontaneously jump into the discussion and yell as loud as you can: "Both of you geniuses—just take off the damned glasses!" The people are so baffled that they stop the argument, and you seize the opportunity to rip the glasses off both of them. There is a moment of great surprise, as both of them for the first time see the sky without colored glasses.

If we are too eager to define the ego, we will be like the man wearing yellow glasses. We will think that the cause of all of our problems is that too many people are wearing red glasses, and thus we need to start a campaign to convince the people with red glasses that what they see is wrong and that they should put on yellow glasses. If they won't be converted to our viewpoint, they must be either controlled or eliminated. If only we can eliminate the view that the sky is purple, we will have solved the problem.

I earlier described how I personally experienced the conflict between Israelis and Palestinians. The problem in a nutshell is that the Israelis are looking at the situation through glasses of one color whereas the Palestinians are looking through glasses of a different color. It isn't just a matter of opinions—it goes deeper in the sense that both sides see something entirely different. Each side is taking the approach that they have to make the other side see what they see. We from the West come into the situation with a different color glasses but being convinced that we are seeing the situation as it really is. We now try to convince both sides to accept our viewpoint—which doesn't reduce the level of tension but only ads to it.

Am I saying there is no way to look at the world that is not affected by the ego? No, I am not. It is possible to look at the world in a way that is not colored by locality, and thus one can see that the sky is blue. Yet even if one sees reality, would it help to go out and try to convince others to accept one's viewpoint? No, because what is the problem here? Is the problem that one man sees the sky as green and the other sees it as purple? The real problem is that both men have a distorted perception. Trying to convince them that what they see is wrong and that they should accept – on faith, as they don't see it – that you are right when you say the sky really is blue simply will not remove the tension.

We need to make people aware that they are wearing glasses that color their perception, and then we need to help them take off the glasses so they can look at life without any kind of glasses. How might we do that? We had better start by making sure that we have taken all of our own glasses off so that we can see reality as it is instead of promoting another colored vision as the one and only truth. This is the main reason we will not rush into defining the ego.

No easy way out

There is another reason for not defining the ego, namely that seeking to define the ego can actually help the ego hide. Another effect of our Western approach to problem-solving is that we want to define everything in concrete terms. When we come up with a concept of an ego, we want to see it as a concrete entity hiding somewhere in the psyche. We want to see it as an entity that has specific characteristics, and we want that these characteristics will not change. The reasoning behind this is that if we can define the characteristics of the ego, we think we will gain power over the ego. However, this can only work if the ego doesn't change.

Here we are touching upon another characteristic of our Western approach. We have a tendency to look for the easy way out. We want to quickly identify a problem or define a scapegoat that is the cause of the problem. Then we declare war on the scapegoat and seek to eradicate it, thinking this will automatically solve our problems. Take for example the war on drugs that seeks to eradicate the drugs and the people who manufacture and distribute them, without even making an attempt to address why people have a desire to escape reality and alter their state of mind.

If we can quickly define the ego as a concrete entity, then we think we will be able to destroy that unchanging entity and solve our problems. The problem is that the ego is not a concrete or unchanging entity. The ego is like a chameleon that will easily change color in order to blend in with the background. If you define the ego as being such and such, it will immediately morph into something else. If we are absolutely sure that we have defined the ego, our definition will prevent us from looking at the morphed ego, meaning it can hide in plain sight as we look at it without seeing it.

I am not hereby trying to make it seem like an impossible task to transcend the ego. I am trying to inject a sense of realism. Overcoming the ego is not and never will be a quick-fix. It is not a matter of defining some concrete, unchanging entity, forcing it out of its cover and destroying it.

Let me give a broad and non-specific description of the ego. Imagine that you take a baby and you put yellow contact lenses on its eyes shortly after birth. The child will now grow up seeing the world through the yellow lenses. Since it has never seen the world without the lenses, it has no frame of reference for even knowing that the world doesn't really look the ways it appears. It will think that the way it sees the world is the *only* way to see the world.

The ego is like a filter that distorts the way we look at the world, yet because we have not – in conscious memory – seen the world without the filter, we have no frame of reference for questioning our perception. Each of us have our own personal filter, and that is why we have conflicts with other people. They are convinced that the world really is the way *they* see it and refuse to believe that the world really is the way *we* see it.

The cave of the ego

This is brilliantly illustrated by the old example of Plato's cave. The Greek philosopher Plato told an allegory in which he described a number of people who were chained inside a cave so they were facing a blank wall. They could not turn around and look through the entrance to the cave but could only see the wall. As people outside the cave would pass by the opening, the sun would project their shadows onto the blank wall. The people inside the cave never saw the real world outside, but only saw shadows on the wall. The people inside the cave could not know what the world outside was like because they could only study the shadows. In order to know reality, the people had to free themselves from their chains and walk outside the cave.

The story also illustrates the role of philosophers or teachers, in that they are the ones who go into the cave and try to persuade the people to take off the chains and walk outside the cave. This illustrates my goal for writing this book. I am not imagining that the people who actually create evil in the world will suddenly decide to read this book, be converted and then engage in a group hug. My real goal is to awaken those who have the potential to serve as teachers or wayshowers.

I have talked about a creative minority, a dominant minority and the majority of the population. I believe the creative minority constitute around 10 percent of the population and the dominant minority another 10 percent, with the population being the remaining 80 percent. The creative minority form the "top 10 percent," meaning that they have the potential to pull society away from the illusion of locality, and thus away from evil. The "bottom 10 percent" of the dominant minority are pulling in the opposite direction, and they are far more aggressive and determined to reach their goals. What is needed is that members of the creative minority are awakened to their potential – and their responsibility – so they will engage in a more conscious and determined effort to pull up the majority. This can be done in two ways:

- All human beings are connected. When you raise your consciousness by exposing and rising above your own ego, you will pull up all other people on this planet. This has already happened with slavery and democracy, and there is no reason to think that it cannot be applied to pulling humankind beyond the mindset that creates evil.

- Any positive step in humankind's journey to our present civilization has been taken because of an increased awareness. When people know better, they will want to do better. The spreading of new knowledge starts with the creative minority whose members act as teachers or examples for the general population.

Those of us who are members of the creative minority are the only ones who have the potential to bring about a positive change. By becoming consciously aware of this and by making a more determined effort, we can have a far greater impact than we have had so far. My goal for this and the succeeding book is to give people both the drive and the tools to engage in this process. For this to work, we have to be willing to follow one of the essential principles for bringing about change, a principle that the ego prevents most people from seeing.

It all starts with me

Those of us who are members of the creative minority have a dream about seeing a better world, meaning we are open to change. However, we are not the only ones. Some of the members of the dominant minority also want change. Many of them even believe that they are working for positive change, even working for a better world. I have talked about an aspiring power elite whose members want to dethrone the established power elite. When Hitler took power in Germany, both he and many of his supporters thought they were bringing about a better Germany, even a better world.

Today, most people realize Hitler's belief was an illusion, and we can now see that Hitler was a text-book example of how the ego can distort people's perception. Many people thought Nazism was based on some higher reality, just as the medieval inquisitors thought they were doing God's work by torturing people or burning them at the stake.

As the old saying goes: "The road to hell is paved with good intentions." The most subtle and fundamental effect of the ego is that it distorts our vision by making us think we are working for a good cause while in reality only increasing the level of tension and conflict in the world.

If we are serious about manifesting a better world, we need to be equally serious in making sure we are not deceived by our own good intentions. You cannot solve a problem with the same state of consciousness that created the problem. If we truly want to solve the problem of evil, we have to be willing to start by overcoming the consciousness that creates evil within ourselves.

This leads us to a fundamental principle: If you want to help the world overcome a problem, you must start by over-coming that problem in yourself. This was expressed beauti-fully and poetically by a wise teacher 2,000 years ago. Read his words as you might never have read them before:

> 3 And why beholdest thou the mote that is in thy brother's eye, but considerest not the beam that is in thine own eye?
> 4 Or how wilt thou say to thy brother, Let me pull out the mote out of thine eye; and, behold, a beam is in thine own eye?
> 5 Thou hypocrite, first cast out the beam out of thine own eye; and then shalt thou see clearly to cast out the mote out of thy brother's eye. (Matthew, Ch 7)

Jesus is actually talking about the ego, as best it could be done with the understanding and vocabulary available at his time. He is saying that we all have a beam – the ego – that dis-torts our perception. This ego gives us the tendency to focus attention outside ourselves and look for the problem in other people. We think that if we can solve the problem "out there" by changing other people, we will have done something for the world. Jesus is saying that this will never work because if we try to solve the problem of the ego with the ego's distorted perception, we will only make things worse. What we truly need to do is to stop looking "out there" and be willing to look for the ego in our own minds. When we have overcome our own distorted perception, we will see clearly and now we can truly go out and help the world overcome the same illusion that we have overcome.

One can argue that most Christians have not followed this, but doesn't this simply prove how subtle the ego is and how persuasively it distorts our perception? For 2,000 years, hardly anyone has understood or followed the deeper meaning in Jesus' statement. Should that prevent us from following it today? I say: "No! Let us be willing to take a closer look at how the ego distorts our own vision before we go out and try to change others. Then we will have the proper foundation for making a real contribution to bringing peace instead of bringing more evil."

8 | THE EGO AND FEAR-BASED EMOTIONS

Why do we so easily see the splinter in the eyes of others yet fail to see the beam in our own eyes? Part of the reason is that unmasking and recognizing the ego is a process that has several stages. At the beginning stage, our challenge is to start seeing the ego and its effects. The more extreme the effect, the easier it is to see it. Most people begin by recognizing the ego in the more extreme cases. Since most people, certainly the people in the top 10 percent, are not prone to extreme forms of egotistical behavior, they have to look to others to see the effects of ego.

By looking at world history, it is not hard to identify the ego at work. It would be a worthy endeavor to expose how the ego has been the driving force behind all of the negative events in history, to write an ego-based history. Adolph Hitler obviously gave us one of the most extreme demonstrations of just how far people can go when they are completely blinded by the ego. Many other historical figures have also displayed extreme forms of egotistical blindness.

Can we find a common denominator? One example is the concept of psychopathic personality disorder, defined by psychologists as a frame of mind dominated by a lack of empathy for others. The ego springs from the illusion of locality, the illusion that we are all separate beings. The more blinded a person is by the ego, the more the person believes in the reality of this separation. The ego makes a person believe that he or she is in a special category, is more important or more right than others. The person has the right to do whatever is seen as needed regardless of the consequences it has for others. In its extreme form, the ego only considers its own goals and has no empathy whatsoever for other people, regardless of how severe is the suffering inflicted upon others. The death of six million people in concentration camps is simply a necessary and justifiable step for accomplishing the goal of purifying the human race.

The actions of psychopaths, mass murderers and dictators clearly spring from the ego. What happens when we go to less extreme forms of behavior? Any form of crime is clearly ego-behavior, in that the criminal is seeking to get an advantage regardless of the consequences it has for others. Only a person blinded by the ego can consider it natural or even possible to steal from other people in order to enrich himself. Only a person blinded by the ego can rape women or molest children in order to satisfy sexual desires.

What if we go to a more personal level? How about people who use any form of physical violence against others, including violence against a spouse or children? How do we define violence? Is it only physical abuse, or is emotional and mental abuse also a form of violence? What about a parent who – supposedly out of concern for a child – becomes overprotective and controlling? Or a parent who did not fulfill his or her dream of a career and now wants a child to do so, even if the child has neither the desire nor the ability?

It is easy to see that any form of behavior that deliberately or knowingly hurts other people is coming from the ego. What about behavior that is not deliberately aimed at hurting others, but is aimed at what the person sees as a necessary goal? If you had asked Hitler, or even some of his close associates, why he was hurting others, he would probably have given you a puzzled look. Even though we might see Hitler's behavior as extreme, he did not see it that way himself. He saw himself working for a worthy goal and probably did not even consider that it hurt others. Many actions that hurt other people are not deliberately or knowingly aimed at hurting others. People are so blind that they do not see or do not consider it important that their actions hurt others.

When we look at the effects of the ego from a superficial perspective, it seems easy to define ego-based behavior. When we start examining the effects of ego more carefully, we see that things are not quite so clear-cut. We now see the need to reach for a deeper understanding.

Ego is more than behavior

Let us imagine that we have a society, such as a large nation or even the Western world, that becomes aware of the ego and learns to identify any negative or self-centered behavior as coming from the ego. This society identifies ego based on behavior. The society now decides that it wants to solve the problem of human evil by getting rid of specific types of ego-based behavior, namely the types of behavior that are seen as generating and sustaining evil.

How would people go about accomplishing this goal? Would they seek to control the behavior of the population by programming children to suppress ego-based behavior? Would they seek to identify people prone to such behavior and then restrain or punish them in order to discourage such behavior? Or would they go so far as to seek to identify certain groups of people as being the cause of ego-based behavior and then either restrain or eradicate those groups of people?

Let me go back to the conflict between Israelis and Palestinians. The Israelis might use the concept of the ego to say that the Palestinians are doing what they are doing because of ego. The world should help the Israelis stop it or let them do it themselves. The Palestinians could just as easily say that the Jews are driven by ego-based behavior. Then the West could step in and say that both are driven by ego and that both need to accept our world view as the superior one.

Identifying the ego and ego-based behavior is a necessary step, but it will not – in and of itself – help us transcend the ego. In fact, the ego might use it to camouflage itself and get people to use the concept of the ego to point the finger at others. People would then be displaying ego-based behavior while thinking they are working for the worthy cause of removing the ego from the planet.

Another danger of identifying the ego based exclusively on behavior is that it will tend to pacify the very people who can do the most to pull society away from the grips of the ego. Imagine that Western society came up with a list of what constitutes ego-based behavior. Many people would look at the list and say: "But I have never done any of those things. Well, that must mean I don't have an ego. So then the problem is with all of those other people who do display ego-based behavior.

We need to change them, not ourselves." All human beings on this planet are connected through consciousness. As the majority of the population goes, so goes society. The majority of the people are followers. They will either be pulled down by the dominant minority toward more self-centered behavior, as we saw the German population being pulled down by Hitler and his collaborators. Or they will be pulled up by the creative minority toward less self-centered behavior, as we have seen many nations being pulled into accepting a democratic form of government based on inalienable rights.

We who want to see a better society can never allow ourselves to define the problem as being "out there" and found only in other people. What Jesus told us 2,000 years ago with the parable about the beam and the splinter is that we will not have a positive impact by focusing on changing other people. We will have a positive impact only by focusing on changing our own consciousness—and thereby pulling up the collective consciousness.

In order to do that, we obviously cannot identify the cause of the problem – meaning the ego – as being only out there. We have to be willing to see it in ourselves because that is the only way we can avoid falling into one of the age-old traps of the ego. This trap is to focus on changing other people instead of first changing oneself, trying to solve the problem by forcing other people rather than first solving the problem in oneself and then seeking to help people from a clearer vision.

Although it is valid to identify the ego as the cause of human evil, we cannot simply identify the ego based on visible actions. We have to go to a deeper level and gain a more sophisticated understanding of the ego. To put it simply, ego affects behavior but ego is more than behavior.

Feeling out the ego

In order to go beyond actions, we only need to ask where actions come from. Many people will say that actions come from thoughts, but is that really true? I once met a man who used to sell vinyl siding (to beautify and isolate wooden houses) in the Seattle area of the United States. Back then, Seattle was dominated by the Boeing Aircraft factory, and the standing joke among salespeople in the area was that nothing was harder than selling to a Boeing engineer. The reason was that the engineers were very intellectual people so for every argument the salesman came up with for why they should buy, the engineer could come up with an argument for why he shouldn't buy. The salesman could argue for hours without being able to get the engineer to make a decision. I am not saying that observation was entirely scientific, but I do believe it illustrates something about the human intellect.

The intellect can argue both sides of an issue very convincingly, which means that the intellect rarely gives us the impetus to take action. Thoughts are somewhat airy, and most of us have many thoughts that we never get around to acting upon. The thoughts stay at the level of ideas and don't make it to the level of action. In order for an action to occur, there must be something besides thought, namely emotion. I am not thereby saying that thoughts are unimportant (as we will soon see), but when you look at the psychological mechanism that triggers an action, the first factor you see is emotions. In order to more fully understand the ego, we have to take a closer look at feelings.

Einstein showed that everything is energy so emotions must be a form of energy. The word "emotion" sounds like "energy in **motion**." Where does the energy of emotions reside? Energy can move through space as a wave or it can be stationary in the form of a field. The mind is – at least in part – an energy field. A magnet has an invisible energy field around it, as does the earth. The human body also has an invisible electromagnetic field around it, and the mind is part of this field. For thousands of years, the ancient healing modality of acupuncture has been based on knowledge of such a field, and today acupuncture is used by many Western doctors and hospitals. We even have technology today, in the form of scanners and digital cameras, that can make the energy field visible on a computer screen. I predict that within the next decades this technology will be developed further and the human energy field will be generally acknowledged and better understood, even to the point that it can be used to diagnose disease before it produces physical symptoms.

The mind as an energy field

By considering the mind as an energy field, we learn something valuable about human evil. One of the basic laws of physics says that energy can neither be created nor destroyed. You can transform one form of energy into another form of energy, and you do so by changing the vibration of the energy waves (frequency, amplitude and wave length). Once you have transformed an energy wave into a certain state, it will remain in that state indefinitely (meaning until an outside force acts upon the energy). Energy will not change its vibration by itself.

An emotion is an energy wave that has a specific vibration. A few scientists have measured the difference in vibration between various forms of emotions, but do we really need scientists to prove that love has a higher vibration than anger?

Our minds have the ability to change the vibration of certain types of energy. When we have an emotion, our minds take a basic form of psychic energy and color or qualify it with the vibration of a specific emotion. When we feel positive emotions, we produce a certain quantity of energy of a higher vibration, and when we feel negative emotions, we produce a quantity of energy with a lower vibration. Our minds can be said to be like a pair of glasses that color the white light that streams through them. If we feel loving, the glasses are pink and if we feel angry, the glasses are red. We color emotional or psychic energy depending on what we feel.

The law that energy can neither be created nor destroyed has a stupendous implication. What happens to the emotional energy we produce; where does it go? The laws of physics make it clear that the energy will not disappear and it will not spontaneously change itself back into a pure state. Once we have qualified the energy with the vibration of anger, it will remain like that indefinitely. In the meantime, it must go somewhere. Emotional energy goes to a place in your subconscious mind. Your physical body has an invisible energy field around it, and your mind either is this field or is connected to the field. The emotional energy your mind qualifies ends up being stored in your personal energy field—in which it will accumulate.

Doctors have for a long time been aware of a connection between people's state of mind and disease. The biologist Bruce Lipton, in his book *The Biology of Belief,* has described how our cells have the ability to respond to our state of mind. Your emotional state can affect your physical health because as emotional energy continues to accumulate in your personal energy field, it will eventually reach such an intensity that it starts affecting the cells.

When you become angry with someone, this produces a certain amount of anger energy that is stored in your energy field. In the following days, you think about the person many times, and each time an additional portion of anger energy is produced—which adds to the accumulation in your field. For a time, all you do is think about what you would like to do, but you cannot quite get yourself to act. After a while, you start feeling a sense of intensity or immediacy, and suddenly you reach a tipping point where you act out against the person. The emotional energy gradually built in intensity until it became such a powerful magnetic force that it literally pulled your conscious mind into acting.

This can be explained by basic science. Everything is energy, and energy is made from waves. When two waves meet, they create what scientists call an interference pattern, which is simply the interaction of the energy waves.

Your conscious mind is an energy field, but it is connected to another energy field, called your subconscious mind. You ideally have control over your conscious mind, meaning that you make a conscious decision concerning how to interact with another person. You do this based on a rational evaluation of what is best for yourself, meaning that you don't do something that will harm yourself or create unwanted consequences in the long run.

When people become angry (or have other negative emotions) they will often act in ways that harm themselves or create long-term consequences. Something takes over their conscious minds so they can no longer make rational decisions—they act on the emotions. The explanation is that when a sufficient amount of anger energy has accumulated in the energy field of the subconscious mind, the energy creates such a magnetic pull on the conscious mind that it overwhelms you and overrides your normal ability to make rational choices. The accumulated energy has now taken over your mind and you are no longer able to act based on reason. This mechanism can explain so many human actions—including conflict and violence on a large scale.

A new view of evil

By recognizing the existence of an energy field, we gain a new view of human interaction, especially evil. Consider that you meet another person and you instantly dislike the person. You have never met the person before and you have not exchanged any words, but the mere presence of that person makes you feel uncomfortable or agitated. The explanation is that when you meet someone, your energy field starts interacting with the field of the other person. If the other person has an accumulation of negative energy, say anger, in his energy field, it will begin to affect your field. It may give you a general sense of discomfort, or it may even activate anger energy accumulated in your own energy field.

Consider that you are having an argument with another person who is blaming you for something, and afterwards you feel either depressed, exhausted or "drained." Again, this can be understood in terms of an exchange of energy between the fields. You have probably experienced that a person was angry with you. Such a person is taking some of the anger energy stored in his or her field and sending it into your field—where it creates a reaction, such as making you feel uncomfortable, agitated or angry. Another possibility is that a person sucks energy out of your field, and that is why you feel drained afterwards—your energies literally have been drained.

Consider the effect on long-term relationships, such as two people who have been angry with each other for decades. Every time they meet, they end up in an argument—even if none of them did or said anything that should have caused a blow-out. Both people have accumulated enormous amounts of anger energy in their fields. The anger has become so intense that it overwhelms their ability to make rational decisions. When they are not together, they seem like normal human beings, but put them together and none of them act rationally. The reason is that both people have accumulated so much anger energy towards the other that they are not having a relationship on the conscious, rational level. Their relationship is entirely driven by the subconscious mind—it is actually their energy fields instead of their conscious minds that are having a relationship. The energy fields cannot make conscious decisions—they can only exchange energy based on what is already accumulated there. It is actually two balls of anger energy that are having an interaction, not two self-aware, rational human beings.

A substantial portion of personal conflicts can be explained by an accumulation of negative emotional energy in people's energy fields. In order to improve a relationship, this emotional energy must be addressed. Imagine what might happen to personal relationships if people became aware of this mechanism and then learned a way to free themselves from the accumulated emotional energy. Long-standing conflicts could literally vanish as if by magic—yet it is not magic. It is simply the increased awareness that has raised us above the past in so many other ways, although not yet in terms of how we deal with emotions.

The collective emotional body

When you enter into a long-term relationship with another person, your energy fields start to interact, even combine. When you live in close proximity to others, such as in a family, the energy fields of all members start combining and creating a collective energy field. When you enter a home where you feel uncomfortable, this is caused by the collective energy field in that home affecting your personal energy field. A dysfunctional family is partly caused by an accumulation of negative emotional energy in the collective energy field of the family. On an even greater scale, we talk about a national consciousness. How is it possible that 300 million people living on a particular piece of land (where someone drew some lines on a map and called it a border) have a national consciousness as Americans? How is it possible that their national consciousness is so distinctly different from that of the 35 million Canadians immediately to their North? If you really want to see the national consciousness in all its glorious variety, go to Europe where people are so alike yet so different.

Consider the collective consciousness of an ethnic group or race. How is it possible that all members of a specific ethnic group can be arguing and fighting with each other, yet when it comes to another ethnic group, they are suddenly united in opposing them.

Such differences at least have a basis in something visible, but then consider religion. People of many different ethnic groups, races or national backgrounds are Christians, and they have a collective consciousness that can see itself as being in opposition to another religious group. Two groups of people may have the same racial, ethnic and national background, but they are still bitterly divided by religion—as the people of Northern Ireland proved not so long ago.

How do we explain that in our modern rational world, two large groups of people can have an ongoing conflict that is so intense that their representatives cannot even communicate? How do we explain that two nations cannot even negotiate about a common policy that would benefit both of their peoples? How do we explain that even at the international level, emotions can still block rational solutions? For example, everyone recognizes that it would be better to have peace in the Middle East. Even the people in the region recognize this and they all say they want peace. Nevertheless, they are so overwhelmed by negative emotions toward each other that they cannot even sit down at the same table to negotiate.

The answer to all of these baffling questions is that there is a collective consciousness. It is an energy field in which all of the negative energy produced by humankind, or a specific group of people, continues to accumulate. Consider the Middle East where people have been fighting for all of recorded history. For thousands of years, people in that region have accumulated anger and hatred so we are talking enormous amounts of energy. That accumulated energy forms a magnetic pull that is so strong it can easily overwhelm most individuals.

What happens to a child that grows up in this atmosphere, for example in the Palestinian part of East Jerusalem? Let us assume that the child starts out being innocent, having no energy in its personal field and having no reason to hate Jews. As the child grows up, it cannot help but realize that all of the adults around it have an intense hatred for Jews. As the child – as is almost inevitable – beings to accept that Jews are bad, what happens to its energy field? The Palestinian people have accumulated a lot of anger and hatred in their collective field. Most of this is expressed as their anger against the Jews, demonstrating our tendency to project that the cause of the problem is outside ourselves.

As the child accepts its parents' view of Jews, it inevitably opens its personal energy field to the collective field. The child is completely overwhelmed by the anger energy in the collective field. The child's mind is literally taken over by the energy in the collective field. Instead of making its own rational decisions about Jews, the child reacts at the level of emotional energy. The child might never have met a Jew or have had any negative encounters with Jews. Its relationship to Jews is not based on reality but on the accumulated emotional energy in the collective consciousness. Of course, an identical mechanism is found in the Jewish part of Jerusalem and in many other places around the world. The longer a conflict has been running, the more energy is accumulated and the harder it is for individuals to avoid being overwhelmed by it.

No reason to feel overwhelmed

I realize what I have explained here goes far beyond what all of us were taught about the world as we were growing up. We were given such an innocent view of the world where there was a clear distinction between good and evil. The evil we see in the world was caused by the bad people, and that is why the good people must fight the bad people. A simple world, but also a world in which conflict and war were seen as unavoidable.

What I am presenting here is a far more complex world view, and I remember my own reaction when I was first exposed to these ideas. I felt a deep sense of hopelessness, almost panic. I felt overwhelmed by the realization of just how much negative energy has been produced by humankind over thousands of years, and it seemed completely hopeless to reverse the downward spirals that have been created. Before, I had thought that people were basically rational and that the right arguments would persuade everyone to make peace. Afterwards, I realized that no amount of argumentation can counteract the pull of the raw emotional energy.

At first, it seemed like there was no way forward. Yet the first step toward overcoming a problem is to recognize and understand the cause of the problem. This will often cause us to think life has become more complicated, but as our understanding increases, we also begin to see ways to solve the problem. The sense of panic, the sense that a problem seems overwhelming, is one of the most powerful effects of the ego, and it forms an emotional catch-22. The term "catch-22" symbolizes a problem that seems to have no solution because there is a paradox that seemingly cannot be overcome.

The emotional catch-22

When I was a young child, I watched a cartoon on television that showed how the skeletons came out of the graves and did all kinds of things, including running into the camera and swallowing you up. Shortly afterwards, my family took me to an excavated medieval monastery that had several graves with real skeletons in them. As a result of these experiences, I developed a very strong fear or skeletons, ghosts and supernatural phenomena. Over time, the fear diminished in intensity, but it was still there when I entered the seventh grade.

At that time, we were allowed to stay in the classroom during recess. We started having biology lessons in a special classroom, and next to it was a large room with no windows that housed the school's collection of stuffed animals and other specimens. Needless to say, it also had a complete human skeleton. It was made of plastic, but life-like enough (pun intended) to trigger my fear.

Sometimes, the teacher would open the room during recess so we could further our education by looking at the specimens. One fine day, I decided that this was going to be the end of my fear. During recess I went into the specimen room along with a group of my classmates. As the next lesson started, the teacher called us out, but I hid behind one of the cabinets. The teacher made the reasonable assumption that everyone was out, and he locked the door from the outside and turned off the light—also from the outside. I was now locked in a completely dark room with a skeleton. I got out from behind the cabinet and

fumbled my way up to the skeleton. As I stood there, I mentally challenged it: "Okay, if you have any power, come get
me now!" After nothing happened, I experienced an emotional
release whereby the last remnants of my fear left me.

This experience taught me a general lesson about life. All
fear is a fear of the unknown, a fear of what we have not faced.
There is only one way to overcome fear, namely to face it and
thereby force the unknown to become known. As long as we
allow our fear to prevent us from looking at the unknown condition that causes it, fear becomes a catch-22, an unresolvable
problem. This is precisely how the ego manages to paralyze us.

Some psychologists say there are only two basic human
emotions, namely love and fear. Love makes you open and
wanting to enter into oneness whereas fear makes you closed,
wanting to move further into separation. Any genuinely positive emotion is an offshoot of love whereas any negative emotion is a variant of fear.

Any negative emotion has the basic dynamic of fear, namely
wanting to close off and withdraw. The effect is that you do
not want to approach and take a look at what you fear—you
want to get as far away from it as possible. All fear is a fear
of the unknown. The only way to overcome fear is to force it
into the open and make it known. Yet the only way to force
it into the open is to approach it—and that is precisely what
any negative emotion makes us want *not* to do. Once we have
allowed an emotion based on fear, we will refuse to look at
the fear, and this becomes increasingly true the more negative
emotional energy we accumulate in our energy fields.

Consider the statement by Franklin Roosevelt: "We have
nothing to fear but fear itself." As a child I read about stone
age people and how they literally believed it was dangerous to
be outside their houses after dark. I also learned about many
other fears that people have had through the ages, fears that

today seem irrational because our knowledge has empowered us to see that there was nothing to fear. What we fear is not an actual condition but something we assume is there without having a direct experience of it.

Our fear is a psychological condition that is created by our imagination, our ability to imagine the existence of something we have not seen. This ability is also what allows us to ask questions about something we don't know. When fear enters the picture, we shut off our willingness to ask questions about our fear. We refuse to question the fear, and thus we cannot free ourselves from the fear and start reversing the accumulation of negative energy. The more we close our minds, the more negative energy we accumulate. The fear has become a catch-22.

If we are to rise above evil, we cannot fall into this pattern of refusing to look at and question our negative emotions. This is especially important because most of us grew up in families and societies that are illiterate when it comes do dealing with emotions in constructive ways. Many of us were exposed to people who never questioned their emotions but allowed them to run their lives, accumulating more and more negative energy throughout life while also directing this energy at others.

Some of us were exposed to people who did question their emotions and refused to direct negative energy at others. Yet their only way to deal with negative emotions was to seek to suppress them, and we can now see why this does not work. Seeking to suppress the expression of an emotion still allows the emotional energy to accumulate, and sooner or later it will reach such intensity that it either overwhelms the person or manifests as deeper psychological problems even physical disease. If we are to develop a better approach to human evil, it is absolutely essential that we develop a better way to deal with emotions that spring from fear.

9 | A BETTER APPROACH TO FEAR-BASED EMOTIONS

I believe that in the not-too-distant future, people will look back at our society and wonder why we had such a glaring omission in the way we educate our children. Why do we focus on teaching children concrete skills, such as "reading, writing and arithmetic" while failing to educate them about the one thing that will affect everything they do in life, namely the human psyche? We bring up our children to be very literate when it comes to the world *outside* themselves, but virtually illiterate when it comes to the world *inside* themselves.

If you take a group of people who are willing to acknowledge that they have fear and ask them what they fear, most of them will point to certain objects or conditions. They will say that the fear is caused by an external object or condition. How does this compare to Roosevelt's insight that we have nothing to fear but fear itself? The object we fear might be outside ourselves, but the fear is not. Fear it not an *external* condition; it is an *internal* condition. It takes place exclusively within the mind itself.

If you ask people how they might overcome their fears, most of them will say that you have to remove or change the object or condition that is causing their fear. The only way to overcome your fear is to change something outside yourself. Is it truly logical that the only way to change an *internal* condition is to do so by changing an *external* condition? Is it really logical that the only way to change a phenomenon that takes place exclusively in the mind is to change something outside the mind? How can we be in control of our lives if the only way to change *internal* conditions is to change *external* conditions? In order to truly be in control of ourselves, we have to find a way to change our minds regardless of external conditions.

Why do we fear a given external condition? There are many external conditions that don't produce any fear. The obvious answer is that there are certain conditions that we perceive as a threat, yet why do we see them as threats? We fear something because we don't have control over it, and thus we fear that it might harm us in some way. We fear something precisely because we cannot control it—as it is either beyond our power to change or dependent upon other people's choices. At the same time, we think the only way to overcome our fear is to change what we cannot control.

How likely is it that we will overcome our fear by trying to change something over which we have no control? How likely is it that we will gain control over our lives if we think our state of mind depends on external conditions over which we have no control? Would it not be far more constructive and logical to take our focus off the external condition and instead take a look at the mind itself? Since fear is an internal condition that takes place in the psyche, the only place to overcome it is by dealing with the psyche itself.

Fear is not caused by external conditions

The ego affects behavior, but it is not enough to identify the ego in terms of behavior alone. There is a link between emotions and the ego, but it would be simplistic to say that the ego is negative emotions. The ego affects our emotions, but it is more than emotion. The ego is something subtle that hides deep within the psyche, and the emotions are part of what allows the ego to hide. The emotions form a kind of veil that hides or camouflages the ego. In fact there is more than one veil.

The first veil we will look at is the illusion that fear (and the negative emotions that spring from fear) is caused by an external condition, such as other people. This illusion is the tendency to identify emotions with the object we fear, thus thinking the only way to change the emotion is to change the object.

Consider the impact that a better understanding of this mechanism could have on human evil. A substantial part of all evil is caused by one person having a fear, but failing to see it as an internal condition, instead associating the fear with another person or another group of people. The person is not seeking to deal with the fear by dealing with his own psyche. Instead, he is seeking to deal with his own fear by forcing other people to change in a way he thinks will alleviate his fear. The other people, of course, see this as an attempt to force them. They resist, possibly because of a fear of their own, such as the fear of being controlled.

History is littered with examples of how this has caused long-lasting conflicts, even major wars, between groups of people. Both groups of people have a fear and both groups refuse to acknowledge the fear as something that exists in their collective minds. They refuse to deal with the fear by looking at the beam in their own eyes, by changing themselves. Instead, they seek to deal with the fear by changing the other group of people, by appointing them as the scapegoat who is the cause of their fear. This leads to an irreconcilable conflict between them—a conflict that will persists as long as both of them refuse to look at themselves.

You may think that Hitler was a very powerful person, but in reality there have been few people in world history who were more controlled by their fears than Hitler. He tied in to a collective fear of the German people, yet instead of recognizing that it was *their* fear, they projected the cause onto the Jews. They then used their Germain efficiency to try to eradicate the scapegoat. There was also the fear of not having enough space – lebensraum – which caused Germany to seek to expand its territory—even seeking to conquer the entire world.

How many other examples of such conflicts can we find? How much suffering and atrocities have been the result of this dysfunctional mechanism of seeking to deal with your own fears by forcing other people to change?

What is the way out? It is to increase our understanding of this mechanism and how it actually limits ourselves. It is easy to look at the second world war and say that the Jews were the victims or that the people attacked by the Germans were the victims. Yet the greatest victims of all were the German people because they became trapped by their own fears and it created a negative spiral that almost destroyed them. Would it not have been far better for the German people if they had become aware of this mechanism so they could have avoided the spiral of allowing Hitler to use their fears to manipulate them into trying to conquer the world? I think the same is true for all people trapped in a fear-based spiral.

The illusion that there is only one way to react

When people fail to realize that all negative emotions are internal conditions that cannot be caused by external conditions, they become very susceptible to the next layer of illusion imposed by the ego. This is the illusion that there is only one way to react to a particular outer condition. We identify the reaction with the circumstances and think that for certain types of circumstances, the only possible reaction is a negative emotion.

We were all brought up to think that the only way to react to certain circumstances is with negative emotions. There is an automatic relationship between *outer situations* and our *inner reaction*. We were brought up to believe that we cannot *choose* our reaction—that we cannot choose to respond with positive emotions regardless of the outer circumstances we face.

Part of the reason we were brought up to believe this is the power elite. The elite can only control the population by controlling peoples' thinking and thereby manipulating their emotions. It is highly educational to watch an old documentary showing Hitler or his propaganda minister Goebbels speak in front of a crowd of 100,000 Germans. Both of them were experts in whipping people into a frenzy in which the individual was overpowered and the crowd became a mob that was willing to follow Hitler to hell and back.

This was done by first playing on people's fears and then turning it into anger that was directed against a clearly defined scapegoat. It now seemed as if the anger was not only justified but the natural response. Hitler's solution of eliminating the scapegoat seemed like the right response. Countless other power elite groups have understood how to manipulate the population by playing on their negative emotions, either by pacifying people through raw fear or by turning fear into anger and then getting them to support aggression against the scapegoat.

Why are people susceptible to the manipulation by an elite? It is because we are already enslaved by our egos. We are enslaved because we were brought up by people who were enslaved by their egos. I am not saying our societies are so controlled by a power elite that they deliberate manipulate every aspect of our upbringing. We have simply grown up in a society where almost everyone shares the illusion that the only response to certain circumstances is negative emotions. As children we emulate the adults around us, and when they were children, they emulated the adults around them. That is how a certain illusion is passed on from generation to generation.

Taking command over your reactionary patterns

Is it really true that if you experience a certain outer condition, your only possible response is a negative emotion? What do you really want in life? You might have certain material goals, such as enough money, the right spouse, a nice house, a rewarding career or something similar. Now ask yourself why you want these things—what do you hope that accomplishing these goals will do for you? Then be even more specific and ask yourself what effect it would have on your state of mind if your goals were fulfilled? As you go through this simple exercise, you will see that your real goal in life is *not* to attain certain *external* conditions. Your real goal in life is to attain an *internal* condition, namely happiness, peace of mind or whatever you want to call it.

What we are all seeking to accomplish in life is to attain a certain *inner* condition. Does it really make sense to say that the *only* – or even the *best* or the *logical* – way to attain an *inner* condition is to attain an *outer* condition? This does make sense to a lot of people, but why does it make sense? It is because these people believe in the illusion that identifies a specific outer condition with a specific emotion. This is one of the key illusions that uphold the personal ego and the collective ego.

If your emotional reaction is inextricably linked to particular outer conditions, then your happiness or peace of mind will always be dependent upon outer conditions. This is not personal freedom; it is not having control over your life. You might get the outer conditions that supposedly make you happy, but you might *not*. Even if you do, the outer conditions are not likely to make you happy. Most of the people in my parent's generation had grown up poor so many people thought that if only they had enough money, they would automatically be happy. Today, many people have more money than they ever dreamed of having, yet they are finding that it doesn't make them happy. The explanation is that happiness is an *internal* condition, and it will only come about when certain psychological conditions are met.

One of those conditions is that you awaken from the illusion that a specific outer circumstance must produce a specific emotional reaction in you. You need to create a space between the outer condition and your emotional reaction so that you have an opening in which you can actually choose your emotional reaction.

The truth we were not brought up to know is that we can choose our emotions. Some of the greatest spiritual teachers of all time have said it is possible for us to choose our emotional reaction. Over 2,500 years ago, the Buddha presented the four noble truths, one of which says that if you approach life with a certain state of mind, then your life will be suffering. By following certain steps, you can rise above the mindset that produces suffering. The path outlined by the Buddha requires you to take command over your emotions so that you can choose *not* to react the way unenlightened people do.

Likewise, 2,000 years ago, Jesus told us that if a person slaps us on one cheek, we should turn the other cheek. What does it require of us to follow this advice? If you take people and slap them in the face, the vast majority of them will go into a negative emotional reaction—and therefore they cannot turn the other cheek. The reaction is based on fear, which causes them to seek to close off and try to avoid another blow. Turning the other cheek is a love-based reaction because instead of closing yourself off, you remain open and give the other person another opportunity to hit you. You can do this only if you are able to choose not to go into the negative reaction that is the default for most people. You must have a space so that after you are hit the first time, you do not react immediately, but you take the time to choose a love-based reaction. In order to do this, you must awaken from the illusion that emotions are caused by external conditions and that certain conditions *must* cause certain emotions. You can accomplish this by seeing through another veil of illusion behind which the ego hides.

Identification with an emotional state

We first looked at the problem that we tend to identify feelings as the effect of an external condition. We then saw that this makes us susceptible to an even deeper illusion, namely that we cannot choose our reaction, we cannot choose our feelings. At an even deeper level is the illusion that our feelings are part of who we are. We identify ourselves based on the emotions and think certain feelings are perfectly natural, unavoidable, justifiable or even constructive.

One obvious example is anger channeled as aggression. Many people in the business world feel this is constructive and the only way to get ahead. Will getting ahead make you happy, or will it only leave you burned out when you can no longer live with the intensity required to stay ahead of the pack? Another example is the feeling of being a victim, of being controlled by others or by life circumstances that you can do nothing about. This can become a way of life, a way to look at life and yourself. You identify yourself as a tough guy or as a victim because you cannot separate your sense of self from the emotional energy of anger or fear.

In order to overcome this illusion, we have to realize that we are *more than* our feelings, that we are *not* our feelings. The only way to accomplish this is to move back the threshold of awareness by looking at our feelings. This is precisely what the ego does not want us to do, and the ego has been very effective in causing the majority of people to avoid looking at their feelings. We grew up in a society where looking at and acknowledging your feelings is considered a social taboo, especially if you are male.

We can break the dead-lock by realizing that emotions can become a catch-22. Because we believe that an external object or circumstance is causing the fear, we think there is no need to look at the fear itself. Fear is a weapon that the ego uses to prevent us from expanding our awareness. By seeing this, we can make a decision that we will no longer allow ourselves to be manipulated by the personal and collective ego. We will indeed do the unpleasant job of examining our emotions.

Some people will run into the problem that the accumulated emotional energy in their energy fields is so intense that they are overwhelmed by the pain. This is a legitimate concern, which I will address in the following book, including presenting a way to decrease the emotional intensity. For now, I am not asking you to actually confront very painful emotions. I am simply asking you to imagine what you will find when you do examine your emotions.

Preprogrammed emotional responses

Emotions can become an automatic or programmed response. When we had to learn how to ride a bicycle, it first seemed impossible to keep the bicycle from toppling over. At some point, it suddenly became automatic. The motor skills required to keep a bicycle balanced had gradually been programmed into the subconscious mind to the point where the subconscious mind could perform the task without us having to consciously think about it. The subconscious mind was now riding the bicycle while the conscious mind could focus on where to go or enjoy the scenery. Obviously, this is a very practical ability that helps us do many things in life, but as with everything else in this world, it also has its drawbacks.

When we have a series of experiences that cause us to react with negative emotions, the subconscious mind becomes programmed to always respond that way. The subconscious mind is subconscious because it is not aware of what it is doing. It is much like a computer, which when you press a certain key on the keyboard will always open up the same window on the screen. The positive effect of this is that it allows us to coast on a bicycle, but the drawback is that it also causes us to coast emotionally.

Once the subconscious computer is programmed to produce a certain emotion as the result of a particular outer stimulus, we have lost our ability to choose our emotional reaction in each situation. Most people have even lost the awareness that we have the ability to choose our emotions. The only way to overcome this programmed emotional response is to move back the threshold of awareness and uncover the program that tells your emotions to respond a certain way. You might begin by considering if there are situations or people who always make you angry, irritated or give rise to other negative emotions. When you see a pattern, you have become aware of an emotional programming. You can then begin to ask yourself whether you really want to react that way and whether you want to be emotionally controlled by this program for the rest of your life.

Many of us developed such programs in childhood, and they were based on our emotional maturity as children. We are now adults so the situations that caused us fear in childhood would not cause us fear today. For example, I no longer feel fear when I see a skeleton. As a child I did, and this built an emotional program that produced fear every time I was exposed to the external stimuli of seeing a skeleton. When I went into the dark room with that skeleton, the program was uncovered and examined. I now created a new program that allowed me to react to skeletons with an adult emotional reaction.

Had I not done that, I would have reacted with fear for the rest of my life. When it came to skeletons I would have been an adult reacting like a child. The vast majority of us still have such emotional programs that were created in childhood. It was perfectly understandable that we created them, as we naturally reacted to difficult situations with the maturity we had at the age of five or eight. Yet we are now adults and would react to those situations with greater maturity. The problem is that we cannot do so until we uncover the childhood program and replaces it with an adult one. It is like never replacing your children's books with books written for adults.

Imagine that you are looking at your emotional patterns, then ask yourself: "I am now looking at my emotions—who is the 'I' that is looking?" You don't actually need to answer that question, you only need to realize that if there is an "I" who is observing your emotions, then the I is not the emotions. You are more than your emotions. By coming to this realization, you can begin to dis-identify yourself from emotions, and this will make it much easier for you to deal with feelings. This will decrease the intensity of your emotions, which will make it much easier for you to move back the threshold of awareness and begin to make conscious choices as to what you want to feel in certain situations. Do you want to feel like a child, or do you want to feel like an adult? Do you want to feel like a "normal" adult or do you want to feel like an enlightened adult?

You will also be able to come to another realization that will allow us to go to the next level in our process of unmasking the ego. You will realize that emotions are not caused by external stimuli. Emotions are caused by thoughts! In order to fully understand the ego, we cannot stop at the level of emotions. We must move on and examine how the ego seeks to hide behind our thoughts.

When you begin to understand fear itself, you realize that all evil relates to fear. So far, the approach that humankind has taken to evil is to identify it with outer conditions and then seek to change those conditions. This is a fundamental part of the collective insanity.

When we understand that fear is not caused by outer conditions, we also see that trying to remove fear by changing outer conditions is never going to work. No matter how much we might change outer conditions, we cannot remove evil from this planet. In order to have a realistic hope of overcoming evil, we have to take our focus away from outer conditions and instead address the psyche itself. Humans are not *biological* beings; we are *psychological* beings. We cannot find viable solutions to our basic problems unless we begin to deal with ourselves and each other as psychological beings. Human evil is produced in the psyche, and it must be overcome in the psyche.

10 | A FEW THOUGHTS ABOUT THOUGHTS

The first line of defense for the ego is to keep us trapped in certain emotional patterns. The purpose of these patterns is to keep us so busy that we have no attention left over to examine our emotions. The ego wants to keep our attention focused on a particular detail so we never step back and look at the big picture, thereby asking ourselves: "Why are we doing this? Why do we continue to do the same thing and expect that any minute we are going to see a different result? If we haven't gotten a different result after thousands of years of doing the same thing, is it time to do something different?"

The key to breaking the emotional catch-22 is to increase our awareness of how emotions limit us by creating conflict between us and other people and unhappiness within ourselves. The key to freeing ourselves from the influence of the ego is to increase our awareness, which means that the main strategy of the ego is to prevent this. The ego always seeks to put us to sleep, and once that has been accomplished, it does not want us to wake up.

When I talk about us being asleep or being unconscious, I do not, of course, mean that we are physically asleep or in a coma. We are indeed conscious, as being conscious is normally defined. Yet we are not truly conscious of what we are doing and what the consequences are—we are focused on conditions outside ourselves and thus cannot find freedom within.

As the ego has created emotional traps or patterns, it has also created a set of patterns that seek to control our thinking—we might call them "thought traps." The ego knows it cannot stop us from thinking so it seeks to keep our thinking within certain boundaries. Our thoughts are like a broken record where the gramophone needle cannot get out of one track. The ego is seeking to create a box in the mind, a mental box, and then prevent us from using our ability to imagine and ask questions in a way that challenges or expands the boundaries of the box. The ego wants to stop us from thinking outside the box. The very foundation for humanity's progress is precisely our willingness to think outside the box. If we want to solve our personal problems, we likewise have to think outside the box.

Imagine that you have a person who has grown up inside an astronomical observatory and has only seen the sky through a telescope. The person has only seen a small slice of the sky, as it is visible through the limited field of view of the telescope. The telescope can be moved around, but it can never give you a full view of the sky. Would such a person have any real appreciation for the beauty of the night sky that one can experience by being outside and seeing the sky in its totality? Would the person have any idea that there was a part of the night sky that could not be seen through the telescope? We have been brought up to see only a small slice of the totality of life. The power elite from without and the ego from within are seeking to prevent us from awakening and seeing the whole picture. They want to keep our thinking trapped in a limited mental box. The power elite can control the population only by staying hidden, and the ego can control the individual only by staying hidden. The only way to stay hidden is to prevent us from thinking outside the box that hides both the elite and the ego. As there were certain layers of emotional veils, there are several layers or veils that limit our thoughts.

Two forms of thinking

Before we look at the specific veils, we will take a closer look at the thinking process itself. The underlying cause of evil is the illusion of locality or separateness, and this illusion has a corresponding form of thinking. There is a certain kind of thinking that springs from and supports the illusion of locality. The goal of the ego is to get us to create a mental box based on locality and then keep us thinking within that box.

Our brains have two hemispheres, and they are said to produce two different ways of thinking. The left brain is the seat of intellectual, analytical thinking whereas the right brain is the seat of intuitive or holistic thinking. The left brain looks at detail and the right brain looks at the big picture. Analytical or intellectual thinking is by its very nature more localized than intuition.

I do not agree that intuition is produced by the right hemisphere of the brain. I see intuition as a faculty that cannot be explained by or limited to the physical brain. I propose that we do not call intuition a form of thinking because, in our Western world, the word "thinking" has become associated with an intellectual, analytical process. Intuition is a more holistic experience that is geared towards having us "see" connections and an underlying unity behind diversity. The intellect is geared towards helping us distinguish, categorize and organize differences. The intellect thinks, or analyzes, whereas intuition "sees" or unifies.

I am not trying to say that there is something wrong with the intellect or that intuition is better than intellect. I hope to raise our awareness of the drawbacks and advantages of each activity so that we can see how this relates to evil. In order to transcend evil, we need to employ both intuition and intellect, and we need to do so in a balanced manner.

Intuition is good at seeing the larger picture and seeing connections, but it is not good at focusing on details. People who have a more developed intuition often are not good at taking care of the practical aspects of life. Likewise, the intellect is very good at dealing with details, but it cannot see the larger picture. It is often said that in the East there was traditionally more right-brain thinking, which is why there was a lower standard of living but a higher satisfaction with life. In the West, there has been more left-brain thinking, which is why we have a very high level of organization but a lower level of general happiness. Precisely because the West has been so dominated by left-brain thinking, we do need to take a closer look at how this form of thinking can be used by the ego to set up mental boxes that make it very difficult for people to see beyond locality.

Locality causes us to focus on what separates us so we overlook what unifies us. The intellect is also focused on differences. This does not mean that the intellect is "bad," is the ego or is necessarily localized. It does mean that it is very difficult to overcome the illusion of locality through the intellect alone. In order to overcome locality, we need to first use our intuition to gain an overall vision of what unites us. Then we need to use our intellects to apply that vision to resolving conflict in the individual, between groups and on the international scale. We need a balance between holistic and detailed thinking in order to both awaken from the collective insanity and have our awakening produce positive change in the practical realm.

We need to consider how the intellect has affected our approach to life—and especially evil. Because the intellect is focused on differences, it can very easily be used by the ego to seemingly affirm the reality of locality. If we rely solely on our intellects – as our Western civilization has a tendency to do – we will never escape locality. The intellect can get us *into* a dualistic mental box, but the intellect cannot get us *out of it*. We cannot think our way out of the collective insanity.

A few words about words

We have now reached a dividing line in this book—a line that will determine whether this book will help awaken you or whether this book will only affirm your existing world view. The issue is that what you have been reading in this book are words. Words are not necessarily localized, but they are distinct, each word having a distinct meaning. The ego can very easily use words to reinforce or confirm a localized view and thereby keep us stuck in conflict.

As an example, take a look at international negotiations. You have representatives from two nations who sit down at a negotiating table to obtain peace, but the only tool they are using is words. What divided them in the first place? Well, not necessarily only words, but you can be sure that words were a part of it. Whatever grievances people have with each other, they will be described in words so a major factor in all human conflict is words. Is there a different way to use words, a way that does not increase conflict but reduces it? If we allow our use of words to be directed exclusively by the intellect, then we will not decrease conflict. The intellect is geared towards categorizing differences, and when it uses words, it uses them in a way that describes and emphasizes differences. This cannot be the basis for transcending evil. When the intellect uses words, it looks at their literal meaning and it cannot go beyond that meaning. There are many examples of this from the world of science and politics, but let me pick an example from the religious world because religion based on the intellect is one of the primary causes of conflict.

Regardless of what you think of Jesus, let us look at what we can learn from his interaction with the scribes and Pharisees. During his brief ministry, Jesus had many conflicts with the scribes and Pharisees and these people were part of the group that had him killed. Most of these conflicts centered around an interpretation of the ancient Jewish scriptures. The scribes and Pharisees tended to interpret the scriptures literally, for example they thought that the command about keeping the Sabbath holy meant that one could do nothing on the Sabbath. When Jesus allowed his disciples to pluck corn on the Sabbath or when he healed a paralyzed man on the Sabbath, the scribes and Pharisees accused him of blasphemy and wanted to stone him. Jesus then made an interesting remark: "The Sabbath was made for man; not man for the Sabbath!"

The intellect simply cannot deal with a remark like that—it is a distinctly intuitive, non-local remark. This statement by Jesus was made with words, but if you interpret it literally – through the intellect – it has no meaning. Take another statement made by Jesus when a young man says he wants to follow Jesus, but he wants to first bury hid dead father. Jesus says: "Let the dead bury their dead." How is the intellect going to deal with a remark like that? Are the corpses going to bury other corpses, but the young man isn't dead so what sense does that make?

To the intellect this is simply "crazy talk," which explains why the scribes and the Pharisees could not handle Jesus and why many modern intellectuals reject everything he stands for. The same goes for the Buddha, who started his main religious scripture with this remark: "Preceded by perception are mental states, for them is perception supreme. From perception they have sprung. If with perception polluted one thinks or acts, suffering follows." Again, the intellect cannot analyze and categorize this so a truly intellectual person is likely to label it crazy talk.

It seems that both the Buddha and Jesus knew the limitations of words and the limitations of the human intellect. They knew that there was no way for them to bring greater peace to earth (the declared goal of both of them) by giving a teaching that appealed only to the intellect. Their use of words seems to be deliberately designed to confound the intellect and have the words activate another faculty of the mind. Both the Buddha and Jesus used words to deactivate the localized form of thinking and propel us into a non-local, intuitive experience.

The original teachings of most of the world's religions use words the same way. This is no guarantee that the followers of such religions will interpret the words in the same spirit in which they were given. The cause of most religious conflict is precisely the tendency to interpret a religious scripture based on the intellect by reading the words of the scripture in the literal way that is the only way the intellect can deal with words.

I recently heard an interview with Karen Armstrong, the author of several books on religion and the religious experience. She explained that the rise of Christian fundamentalism was a phenomenon that came about after the rise of science. Fundamentalism was a result of the scientific, intellectual way of thinking being transferred to the field of religion. This made people think that the Bible must be interpreted literally (as if any "interpretation" could ever be literal). It is interesting that fundamentalism is extremely hostile toward science and materialism, yet based on the same form of thinking as scientific materialism.

Let us be more direct and consider your experience of reading this book. If you read a work of fiction or poetry, you might shut off the intellect and not take the words literally. This is a non-fiction book, and most people tend to read such books based on intellectual, analytical thinking. If you have read this book with the intellect alone, it is likely that you have found that you disagreed with a number of the points I have been making. You might have had intellectual arguments against what I was saying, and these arguments seemed more valid to you than mine, thus you disagreed with my conclusions. I expect that some people will have found one conclusion they disagreed with so strongly that they used it to reject the entire book.

There is a different way to read this book, and that is to use your intuitive faculty to go beyond the literal meaning of the words. You are not reading the book at the level of words— you are not seeing the words and their literal meaning as an end in itself. You see the words as mere signposts that lead you beyond the level of words to a holistic experience, and intuitive experience, an "Aha-experience."

One of the major factors that creates conflict is that we human beings use words in different ways and we attach different meanings to the same words. If you read this book only with the intellect, it will not help you awaken from the collective insanity and it will not help you become a force for decreasing human evil. On the contrary, it will annoy you and this only contributes to evil.

Understanding analytical thinking

Albert Einstein is often considered to be one of the most intelligent people who ever lived, yet he was keenly aware of the limitations of the human intellect. He did not discover the theory of relativity as a result of intellectual thinking. He "saw" the basis for the theory in an intuitive vision as he was riding a trolley car on his way home from work. It then took him two years of work with the intellect to formulate his vision as a credible scientific theory.

Einstein said: "The most beautiful thing we can experience is the mysterious. It is the source of all true art and all science. He to whom this emotion is a stranger, who can no longer pause to wonder and stand rapt in awe, is as good as dead: his eyes are closed." What Einstein called the "mysterious" is not the result of intellectual analysis but the product of an intuitive, holistic experience that is beyond what we normally call thinking.

The intellect thinks through analysis, and according to the dictionary, analysis is a process of breaking a topic or object of study into smaller parts in order to get a more detailed understanding of it. Analysis is designed to give an understanding of detail rather than the whole. Again, there is nothing inherently wrong with this, and it has indeed enabled science to gain a deeper understanding of how things work. Because intellectual analysis has been so successful in helping us build technology, it has obscured the larger picture, such as whether we *should* do what is technically possible. There is even a deeper question of whether technology can ever make us happy and fulfilled.

Analytical thinking has also caused us to focus on how things work rather than what they are. Scientists can describe how energy behaves but have no answers as to what it is. The same, incidentally, holds true for a phenomenon we experience daily, namely electricity. No scientist can tell you what it is; only what it does. Again, analysis is specifically designed to help us categorize obvious or visible differences rather than seeing underlying or invisible connections.

Given that analytical thinking is based on categorizing differences, can analytical thinking help us find a unifying element that will allow us to see beyond human evil? The answer is most likely a "No," and we can see this by taking a closer look at the analytical process.

The basis for analysis is to break a topic into smaller parts, meaning that it looks at the trees and overlooks the forest. Take a topic such as "life." This is a topic that is far too broad for the intellect to deal with. The intellect must break it into a number of more specific categories and then study each of those as separate, independent and possibly unconnected topics. Science has been divided into a number of branches that have become so specialized that there is no unifying vision behind them. The more specialized science becomes, the more difficult it becomes for scientists from different disciplines to communicate with each other. Hardly anyone is looking at all the disciplines and seeking to fit them into a larger whole. Everyone is so focused on studying the individual trees that there is no unifying vision of the scientific forest. Some scientists even deny that there is a forest.

How the intellect intellectualizes

How does the intellect process information? It creates what is similar to a file cabinet or database, only it is located in our subconscious minds. This database has a number of separate file folders or categories, each one with a distinct label. Information is sorted into the categories based on predefined criteria.

These criteria are defined based on analytical thinking, meaning they are designed to break information up into smaller units. This breaking up process is accomplished by focusing on the differences and sorting the information based on differences.

Let us look at a practical example. How does the intellect deal with a subject of study called "human beings?" First, it will categorize us as a life-form on earth. In doing this, it must have already created a database that contains a number of criteria. For example, the intellect must have a way to distinguish between what is a life-form and what is just a form. It must have a way to distinguish conditions on earth from conditions on other planets with no life. This is based on determining the differences between earth and other worlds and between living beings and non-living forms.

The next level would be for the intellect to compare humans to other life forms on earth. Again, the intellect must create categories. For example, one category is that of mammals, defined as life forms that are different from fish in specific ways. Even the category of mammals must be divided into subcategories, and humans are fit into the subcategory of primates. Even there, we are set apart from other primates due to specific differences.

So far this is all practical stuff, and although it can be said to be based on differences, it is not necessarily based on the illusion of locality. We live in a world of form, meaning that the world is composed of a number of distinct forms. These forms are distinct because they have differences, for example a square is different from a circle. There is nothing inherently wrong with the intellect analyzing distinct forms and organizing them into categories based on their differences.

"Human beings" is a very broad object of study, and the intellect can deal with it in only one way, namely by breaking it into smaller parts based on differences. When the intellect looks at human beings, its modus operandi is to detect any differences and then divide people into categories. One obvious category is sex. There are two human sexes, and there are some obvious physical differences between them. The intellect can go further and can detect psychological differences between men and women.

Another difference that the intellect can easily identify is that of race. Based on skin color and certain physical traits, human beings can be divided into a number of racial categories. The intellect can begin to come up with psychological differences between such categories, including – as some prominent scientists have actually stated publicly – that certain races are inferior in intelligence to the white race. Right here I think we can all begin to see how the intellect's tendency to divide us up based on our differences has set the stage for the emergence of evil.

I want to make it clear that I am not trying to say that it is the intellect that creates evil. By dividing us up into separate categories based on differences (real or perceived), the intellect does set the stage for the ego to induce seemingly irreconcilable conflicts between the different categories of human beings. We will shortly take a look at how this works, but first I want to explore how analytical thinking is related to emotions and actions.

11 | INTELLECT, EMOTIONS AND ACTIONS

I would like to avoid any conflicting views about our origins. I think most of us can agree that at some point in the past, our forefathers lived as hunters who found their food in forests where they could be attacked by dangerous predators. Imagine one of your forefathers walking through a dense forest. Suddenly, he spots a movement out of the corner of his eye. This could potentially be a predator that is ready to kill him, or it could be a game animal that will give him his next meal.

His life could literally depend on his ability to detect the differences between the movement of a predator or game animal—and he needs to be able to detect that difference in a split second. Within the same time frame, he also needs to be able to determine the appropriate response and execute that response. This process of detecting the differences, determining the cause of the movement, selecting the response based on past experiences and executing the response needs to happen so quickly that there is no time for a conscious process of analysis and evaluation. The conscious mind is simply not fast enough to ensure the survival of our forefather. He who hesitates – in order to think consciously – is lost.

We can now detail the process that takes place below the level of conscious awareness. The eyes of our forefather registered movement (incidentally based on differences and contrast) and sent a signal to the brain. Here, the intellect compared the sensory input to the subconscious database. With lightning speed, it analyzed the distinct form of the input, compared it to the database and picked the category that matched it most closely. Let us say the intellect found the closest match to the category labeled "Predator." The intellect then looked inside the category for a predefined response based on how our forefather had dealt with similar situations in the past. There may have been several possible responses, but based on its analysis, the intellect selected the one that seemed most appropriate and then sent an impulse to the emotions. This impulse almost instantly sent a surge of fear through the emotional body and the effect was to activate the muscles.

All of this happened so fast that the conscious mind probably only registered the thought "Predator" and felt the emotion of fear. The muscles of the body had already started producing an evasive maneuverer of either climbing a tree or running away. If the intellect had determined that the predator was too close for escape, the body might have taken a defensive stand.

All of this happened beneath the threshold of conscious awareness. Our forefather did not make a conscious analysis of the situation, and he did not make a conscious decision as to how he would respond to the situation. Had he done so, he would have been dead, and then he would not have been our forefather. He responded to the situation from the level of the subconscious mind.

How we respond without conscious thought

How does this relate to human evil? Let us go back to the Palestinian man I described earlier. I asked him: "What happens if the Jews destroy the Dome of the Rock?" His response was: "It will be World War III." This response was not the result of a careful or conscious analysis. It was what we might call a gut reaction, and it is tempting to label it as an emotional response. Yet the response did not originate at the level of emotions. The response originated at the level of thought, and it came from the person's subconscious database—the database that was created and is used by his intellect.

I provided the input, and the essence of it was "Jews," "Dome of the Rock" and "destroy." His intellect immediately – and below the level of conscious awareness – took this input and compared it to its database. There was a category labeled "Jews" and it contained all of this man's prior experiences with, thoughts about and feelings for the Jews. To be fair, this man was not entirely negative towards Jews, but there was definitely some history that in certain situations would portray the Jews as a threat. This became combined with what the intellect found in the "Dome" category, namely that this is the third-most holy site in Islam, which is the only true religion and thus it is of epic importance to preserve the religion and its holy sites. Already here we see that the intellect selected the most threatening subcategory from the category for Jews and it then started looking for a response. In order to do this, it looked in a third category for punishment and because it judged the threat to be maximum, it selected the response that seemed most extreme, namely "World War III." This happened subconsciously because the response to my question was almost instantaneous.

This shows how a normally fair-minded and balanced man was propelled into a highly emotional response in a way that completely bypassed his conscious mind. In fact, he looked downright surprised at what he had just said. A lot of conflict springs from and is maintained by exactly this kind of gut reaction. We cannot get beyond this reaction by dealing with the emotional level. We have to acknowledge that emotions spring from thoughts and then we have to examine where the thoughts come from. When we have identified the thoughts that lead to conflict, we have to look beyond them to thoughts that can unify us rather than divide us.

This is where we need to go beyond the intellect. The intellect – by its very nature – is designed to categorize and organize differences. It is even designed to select a response based on differences. While such a response is clearly appropriate in some situations, this response cannot form the basis for resolving conflict. We will never awaken from the collective insanity through intellectual analysis alone. The awakening requires us to see beyond differences, something that the intellect is not designed to do.

We need to step back and take a look at our subconscious databases, identify how they lead to conflict and then revise our databases – both the categories and the information in them – in such a way that we can respond to each other without conflict and aggression.

The need to find a new approach to conflict

Part of what causes the collective insanity and makes it so difficult for us to overcome evil is our subconscious databases. Our personal databases contain categories that organize what we know about life, but also our feelings about life. The database contains our previous experiences and our existing knowledge, but because it is organized and maintained by the intellect, it tends to focus on differences. When we face a given situation, our subconscious minds will analyze the situation and look for similar situations in the database. If it finds a match, it will look for a response to the situation based on what we have done in the past. The energy that has accumulated over time can have a major impact in terms of selecting our response. The more anger energy is stored, the more likely it is that we will respond with anger.

This may seem like a simple or even innocent mechanism, and it is. But it also has some potentially enormous consequences. Once a certain view of a situation has entered the database, it tends to become self-sustaining or even self-reinforcing. After a pattern of behavior has been established, we tend to repeat that behavior in any situation that seems similar to what we have encountered in the past. If we have established a conflict between two individuals or two groups of people, it can be very difficult for people to overcome the conflict. When a conflict goes beyond a certain point, a negative spiral forms and the energy can have such a magnetic pull on the minds and emotions of the people affected that they do not have the mental power to pull themselves out of it.

Again, let us look at the relationship between Palestinians and Jews. Most Palestinians have a category in their subconscious databases labeled "Jews," and, of course, most Jews have one labeled "Palestinians." The content of these categories is determined by what the individual knows about, thinks about, feels about and has experienced with the other group. It is also tied to what the group has experienced over its long history. Once a certain amount of negativity has entered the category, it will color the person's view of other people. It now becomes likely (even inevitable) that one group will respond to the other group based on a pattern in the subconscious database rather than responding to people or situations on an individual basis.

For example, if a Palestinian hears about a Jew who has been unkind to a Palestinian, this will be seen as reinforcing the generally negative view of Jews. If that same Palestinian hears about a Jew who has been kind to a Palestinian, it is likely to be dismissed or labeled unimportant. The first incident confirms the already accepted view and is accepted without any further scrutiny. The latter incident contradicts the already accepted view and is dismissed without any further scrutiny. The effect is that the database has now become a closed system based on selective processing of information. Information that confirms the existing view is allowed in. Conflicting information is filtered out or labeled as unreliable or unimportant.

The inevitable result is that once tension has reached a critical point, it can only build because the selective information processing reinforces the conflict. Once a critical point has been reached, it is likely that violence will be seen as the acceptable response, even as the default response or the only possible response. A situation that otherwise would not have resulted in violence will now lead to violence. The response is not based on the incident itself but on the entire history and emotional momentum stored in the subconscious databases of the two sides. It now becomes entirely possible that a Palestinian would respond with violence in a situation involving Jews whereas if the same situation had involved other Muslims, the reaction would not have been violent. Of course, the same pattern can be seen in how Jews, even the Israeli state, responds to Palestinians.

Once a negative spiral has been formed, peace cannot be brought about unless we make a deliberate and conscious effort to brake the spiral. We must be willing to examine the categories in the subconscious database and their content. We must be willing to acknowledge that the database is based on differences, and then we must reach beyond them for a view of the situation and each other that is focused on what unifies rather than divides us.

What happens when you put Palestinians and Jews together at the negotiating table? You have very strong emotions that can lead to such negative reactions that the two sides cannot even talk. We will never get beyond the emotions unless we realize that they come from the thoughts and experiences stored in the databases. Even then, we must realize that the databases are based on intellectual analysis that is focused on differences. The two sides will have completely different views of the situation because they are seeing the same situation through different filters. None of them have a unifying view of the situation; they have a view focused on differences. They will keep doing the same thing while expecting the other side to do something differently, and thus they will remain stuck in the collective insanity. We once again see the need to become more conscious of how our minds limit us, which is why we will take a closer look at the subconscious mind and how it works.

How do we recognize a good idea?

What happens when you experience a new situation, come across a new idea or is presented with new information? Your intellect's first task is to compare it to the categories in the database in order to determine in which category it fits. The intellect is comparing everything new to the contents of its database—to what it already knows. It is then seeking to label the new by comparing it to what is already known. Once again, there is nothing inherently wrong with this. The potential drawback is that we will label something new based on what we already know. If the new idea is fairly close to what we already know, this is not a problem because the idea will fit in one of the existing categories in the database. The intellect will simply label the idea and fit it into the right file folder. This is what we call an incremental expansion of knowledge. It can be very useful, but it can also have a very subtle limiting effect on our thinking.

As an example, take what happened in the field of physics before Einstein. In the late 1800s most physicists and chemists believed science had made all of the major discoveries that could possibly be made. Scientists thought they had discovered the basic mechanisms that determine how the universe works, and all that was left to do was to fill in some minor details. Scientists believed that all that was left was an incremental expansion of their existing knowledge. They believed they had created all of the categories that were needed in their database, and all that would be discovered from then on would fit into the existing categories in the database.

There were two drawbacks to this belief. One was that scientists were not looking for any new discoveries, meaning that they were not willing to question their existing categories or look beyond them. Most believed there was nothing beyond those categories. This hindered scientific progress because no mainstream scientist was willing to ask questions outside the box or database of existing scientific knowledge and the world view based on it. This is precisely why it took a non-mainstream scientist to ask such questions and thereby discover the theory of relativity—which took science to an entirely new level.

The second drawback to the belief that everything new will fit into our current database is that when Einstein did present his new theory, many mainstream scientists at first rejected it.

Some even called it a Jewish plot to take over the world of science (this is not a joke). If we allow the intellect to dominate the way we deal with knowledge, we will not be looking for new ideas, and when we do come across them, we often tend to reject them.

In his classical book *The Structure of Scientific Revolutions* Thomas Kuhn describes the progress of science as a twofold process. One aspect is the incremental expansion of knowledge driven by intellectual analysis. This process fills in the existing categories in the database based on the existing paradigm or world view. This process can only take progress so far. Once in a while there is a need for a revolutionary leap that challenges the old world view and opens up for a new view. This will create new categories in the database and open up new fields of inquiry.

The process that has brought us forward has followed this pattern. The intellect has been a valuable tool in this process, but if we had used only the intellect, we might never have made it beyond the leap from hunter-gatherers to an agricultural society, or from agriculture to the industrial revolution, or from totalitarianism to democracy, etcetera.

The intellect itself cannot bring about revolutionary leaps. The explanation is that the intellect is designed to detect, label and organize information based on differences. It is not designed to see connections between distinct pieces of information, nor to see an underlying pattern that can put distinct pieces of information into a unifying framework.

If we want things to remain the way they are (until we blow ourselves up, destroy the environment or create some other calamity), then all we need to do is to continue to allow the intellect and the subconscious mind to determine how we deal with new ideas. The basis for progress is to find a new idea, a new way to look at the old problems. Which part of our minds can recognize and act upon a new idea? Neither the intellect nor the subconscious mind can do this—only the conscious mind can do this.

The conscious mind can only act upon an idea when the idea actually reaches the level of the conscious mind and is recognized as something that requires us to act. If we are not aware of how the intellect and the subconscious mind work, then it is quite likely that new ideas will be filtered out before they reach the level of conscious awareness. We reject ideas without consciously thinking about them.

12 | HOW OUR MINDS FILTER OUT INFORMATION

You might think that if you read about a new idea, surely your conscious mind will be aware of it. Let us take a closer look at how our minds actually work.

I am going to ask you to look up from this book and take a quick look at your surroundings, then move your eyes back to the book and read on.

Now ask yourself (without looking) what objects you saw, how many of each kind, what was their color and internal positions. Now look up again and see how well you did.

Did you notice something from the second look that you did not notice at first glance? You probably did, and this shows us something essential about how our minds work. When you took that first peak, your eyes registered everything that was visible around you—yet your mind did not take note of everything that the eyes detected. I am deliberately not saying that your eyes "saw" everything. Your eyes are mechanical instruments that detect light waves; it takes your mind to actually "see" something. Seeing is a process of converting input into information—and only the mind can produce information.

Your eyes produce a lot of input that is not noticed by your conscious mind. Your subconscious mind has a process whereby it filters out some of the input from your eyes and only presents to your conscious mind the input that meets certain criteria. A similar process applies to all input. We live in what has been called the "information age," and we are daily bombarded with so much new information that our conscious minds cannot deal with it. We cannot consciously evaluate all of the information that comes at us. In order to avoid being overwhelmed, we have set up a subconscious process that filters the information, presenting to our conscious minds only what meets our predefined criteria.

The faculty of the mind that takes care of filtering information is the intellect. We are filtering information based on dividing it into two main categories, namely information that requires our conscious attention and information that does not—at least not right now. The part of the mind that is designed to divide something into smaller units based on differences is the intellect.

Again, there is nothing inherently wrong with this process. It works very well when it comes to factual information. When it comes to concepts and ideas, we have a potential problem, especially when it comes to the kind of unifying, non-local ideas that can bring about a revolutionary leap.

The intellect has one overall goal. Its task is to process all input that comes to you before it reaches the conscious mind. The intellect functions as the gatekeeper or protector for the conscious mind. When the intellect is presented with a new idea, the overall goal is to fit it into its existing database. The intellect attempts to accomplish this by analyzing the idea, meaning that it seeks to break it into smaller components

based on finding differences. The intellect then seeks to compare these components to the categories of its database with
the goal of fitting the new information into one of the existing categories. If possible, it will even seek to determine the
appropriate response to the idea based on what you have done
in the past.

A non-local, unifying idea cannot be broken into smaller
components without loosing its revolutionary potential. An
idea that can revolutionize your thinking cannot be fit into
your existing database categories. Once it fits into your existing
mental box, it cannot take your thinking beyond that mental
box. This is precisely why our mental boxes become closed
systems and we get stuck in repeating the same old patterns
indefinitely—perpetuating the collective insanity. We can't
stop doing the same thing because we can't stop thinking the
same way.

When you are presented with an idea that is too far beyond
your existing world view, it is entirely possible that the intellect
will filter out the idea and use your existing database to label it
as not needing your conscious attention. If you truly want to
awaken from the collective insanity, you have to become more
aware of how you deal with new ideas.

Can the intellect think?

Can the human intellect actually think? I earlier said that the
intellect thinks and intuition sees, but let us look at a practical
example.

Your physical eyes are the foundation for your reading of
this book, but are your eyes reading the words on the page?
In reality, your eyes simply process light rays and turn them
into signals that are sent to the visual cortex in the brain. Your

eyes do not "see," meaning they do not even see the words. Your eyes process input in the form of light rays, but your eyes cannot impose a pattern on the light rays and call them words. Your eyes detect black dots on a white background, but they cannot organize the dots into a pattern that forms words.

It is your brain that imposes such a pattern on the signals it receives from the eyes and then turns the pattern into distinct words, each with a particular meaning. Even though each word has a distinct meaning, the words are combined into larger units, called sentences or paragraphs. These units can convey a meaning that is far beyond the individual words.

Consider the almost miraculous process whereby black dots on a piece of paper are converted into light rays, that are converted into signals sent to the brain, that are converted into words, that are again converted into very abstract ideas. This is truly an amazing leap from something very concrete to something entirely abstract. At which point during this process does the concrete signals become abstract information?

Let us examine a popular myth that many people have come to believe, namely that computers can think. Helped along by popular movies, many people think computers have some kind of awareness. I have even heard prominent scientists claim that computers store and process information. This has given rise to the popular dream of one day creating computers that can think like humans, what is called artificial intelligence (a term that never causes people to ask what *natural* intelligence might be).

I am right now typing these words on a computer. Many people will say that since my sentences contain information and since they are stored by the computer on the hard drive, the computer is obviously storing information. In reality, what gets stored on the hard drive is electronic signals that take only two forms, namely on and off. The computer can convert these on-off signals into the numbers 0 and 1, and it can then organize these two numbers into specific sequences. Each such sequence is called a "byte," but technically this is not *information*—it is *data*.

The information in this book might be stored on my computer's hard drive, but to the computer it only appears as data. The computer has absolutely no idea what information is stored in the data on its hard drive. It can find a particular bit of information, but it does not do so by recognizing it as information. It only does so based on recognizing the pattern that is used to organize the on-off signals into units. The computer does not store *information;* it stores *data*. Data has no meaning in itself and the computer has no awareness of what is stored on its hard drive.

When does data become meaningful? Not when it is displayed on the computer screen, but only when *you* look at it. A computer deals only with data and the computer does not have the awareness to turn the data into information. Only a conscious mind has that ability, and as of this writing no machine has the necessary level of consciousness. This is even proven by quantum mechanics, which has shown that until a conscious mind becomes involved, an observation has not been made and no information has been acquired.

If you want proof, open your Internet browser and type the following: "Find any joke that you think is funny." Any child who can read and write can perform this task, but a computer cannot because it does not have the awareness to find anything funny. It can find the words "joke" or "funny" but it cannot determine whether the data it finds is actually funny. Did you ever search for jokes and hear the computer chuckle as it presented the results?

I fully understand that for many people this is a hard illusion to let go of. The reason is that there seems to be so many similarities between computers and humans. Many people do seem to think just like computers. The reason is that our intellects actually think like computers—or rather computers think like our intellects because they were designed to do what the intellect does. It was the intellect that designed computers to process information the same way it does.

How our brains and minds deal with information

Your eyes detect light rays that it converts into signals that are similar to the on-off signals used by a computer. Your physical brain then imposes certain patterns upon these signals, thereby organizing them into units that are similar to the data stored by a computer—comparable to the individual words. Then your mind – specifically the intellect – converts this raw data into a more sophisticated form. The intellect can attach a form of meaning to the data. The intellect then uses this meaning to organize the data, but is what the intellect organizes actually information and is the intellect actually thinking about it?

There is a long-standing discussion among quantum physicists about when a measurement has been made. If you set up a Geiger counter to detect a subatomic particle, does the machine make an observation? Some physicists say that the machine only records data and that it only becomes information when a conscious mind enters the measurement situation. I suggest that when the intellect is allowed to work beneath the level of conscious awareness, it is not actually processing information—it is merely processing a form of sophisticated data. As long as the intellect works beneath the level of conscious awareness, the intellect is not actually thinking.

I would even suggest that the intellect cannot think by itself. The intellect is a mechanical faculty designed to help us process large amounts of data, selecting the data that our conscious minds need to think about and storing the rest in the subconscious database for future use. The intellect is also designed to help us respond to situations that require such quick actions that our conscious minds would be too slow.

If we allow our intellects to select all of our responses to life, then we are not truly conscious and we are not truly thinking beings. We have reduced ourselves to a form of mechanical beings, a form of biological robot, whose mental processes are only slightly more sophisticated than those of a computer. This might be the mental state that Jesus talked about when he said: "Let the dead bury their dead!"

In contrast, when we go beyond this stage, we can become truly self-aware beings who are fully alive. In that state of mind, the intellect is a very useful tool, but it is only a servant; not the master of our mental processes. Our conscious minds can then use the intellect to organize the kind of information that the intellect can deal with, and it can use the intellect to work out and implement practical changes.

Our conscious minds can also use our intuitive faculties to deal with ideas that the intellect cannot easily process. We can raise ourselves beyond the illusion of locality, awakening from the collective insanity and presenting a viable alternative to human evil. For this to happen, we need to understand how the ego makes use of the intellect and its way of processing data.

Why the intellect cannot make moral decisions

Why is it that the intellect has not produced world peace or resolved moral and ethical problems? Over the years, many intellectual people have attempted to bring peace in conflict situations, but they have rarely if ever succeed. Likewise, we see that intellectual people can sometimes commit amazingly insensitive actions, such as developing destructive weapons, technology that destroys the environment or performing inhumane medical experiments on animals or even people. It is a common observation that intellectual people often find it difficult to make decisions about moral or ethical issues, and we can now see an explanation.

The intellect is not truly thinking, and it is not actually processing information. The intellect only deals with sophisticated data, and although it can distinguish between different types of data, it attaches no deeper meaning or significance to the data. More specifically, it attaches no moral or ethical significance to the data, and that explains why people who rely mainly on the intellect find it difficult to make such decisions. They cannot say that one idea or one course of action is more "right" than another because to them both options seem equally valid or important. Let us look at a historical example.

Many people are familiar with the "Mad Scientist Syndrome," yet few people know that it started with Einstein. It was Einstein's theory of relativity that built the scientific foundation for developing a nuclear bomb. During the second world war, Einstein was living in the United States and he was asked to lead the Manhattan project, the secret project to develop a bomb. He refused to even participate in the project, and if you study his life, you see that he did not do so based on an intellectual analysis. He did so based on an intuitive sense that this was morally wrong.

Another scientist, Robert Oppenheimer, then accepted the position and the project resulted in plunging the world into the era of potential nuclear annihilation. Oppenheimer was the typical intellectual, and he was indeed the basis for the Mad Scientist Syndrome, as illustrated in the movie, *Doctor*

Strangelove. Oppenheimer was a highly intellectual person, and to the end of his life he felt that developing the nuclear bomb was fully justified. He did this based on a line of intellectual reasoning. The problem is that for each of Oppenheimer's arguments, it is possible to present a counter-argument. From a purely analytical viewpoint, it is impossible to say which line of reasoning is more right than the other.

The intellect cannot actually make decisions. The intellect analyzes, which means that it can present arguments both for or against any question. The intellect cannot in itself decide which argument is more right or valid than another, meaning that the intellect cannot make a decision to implement one over the other. That is why many intellectual people are indecisive when it comes to moral or ethical matters and why they are rarely successful in politics.

The human intellect is not the cause of human evil. Intellectuals can rarely make the decision to take decisive or violent action, simply because the intellect cannot tell them what is right. At the same time, the intellect cannot pull us out of evil or conflict. Once a conflict has been started, an intellectual person will keep doing the same thing indefinitely because he cannot pull himself out based on moral or ethical concerns. If an intellectual person has been convinced of the validity of a purpose, he will develop a nuclear bomb, a chemical weapon or even a virus that can kill all human beings on earth. He will also continue to kill whales or cut down rain forest as long as it is profitable to do so.

What aspect of the mind allows us to make moral and ethical decisions—and allows us to take immoral and unethical actions? We have two options for making such decisions:

- We can base them on intuitive, non-local insights.

• We can base them on the localized mental state produced by the ego.

We will later take a closer look at intuition, but for now I want to focus on how the ego can use the intellect's way of processing information to manipulate us into making unconscious "decisions."

How the ego gets us to make unconscious decisions

What should ideally happen when you are presented with an idea that does not fit into any of the categories in your subconscious database? Ideally, this is when you go beyond the automatic response of letting the intellect brake down the idea until it fits into your existing mental box. Instead, you take a creative look at the idea, and here are a couple of the creative responses:

• You create a new folder in your subconscious database so that similar information can be stored there. This is not all that creative, and it does come with the danger that the idea can be ignored for a long time. Yet sometimes an idea really isn't clear enough to warrant further action, and creating a new file folder is better than breaking the idea down until it fits into existing folders. By creating a new folder, you have a place to store similar information until you have so much that it becomes possible to take further action.

• You evaluate whether this new information warrants that you make changes in how you look at life or how you respond to certain situations in life. You take a critical look at the categories in your subconscious database, and you pull the data stored there into conscious awareness. You then evaluate your existing knowledge and perhaps throw away incorrect knowledge or modify it based on the new information. You also evaluate any old patterns or habits that normally determine your response to certain situations. The new information might make it necessary to reject some of these patterns or create new ones.

If you monitor your emotional and mental reaction to what you have just read, you might discover a certain resistance: "This sounds very complicated and it would be a lot of work." You might notice an even more extreme reaction of feeling threatened by my suggestion, and the range of reactions will go from the lazy to the openly hostile. This reaction comes from your ego—plain and simple.

As we have seen with emotions, your ego wants to set up certain patterns, and then it wants you to stay within the framework defined so you never go beyond it. Likewise, the ego wants to set up patterns for how you think about life, and then the ego wants you to stay in that mental box. If something happens that requires you to think outside the box, the ego will seek to discourage you in all ways possible. This is the resistance you just felt.

Consider how this relates to resolving conflict. The two sides in a conflict have created a category in their databases for how they see the other side and how they are supposed to respond to the other side. How could the conflict possibly be overcome? Only by both sides being willing to take a conscious look at their databases and revise their views of each other and their habitual responses. As long as the people resist this conscious, creative thinking, the conflict will continue, sometimes for thousands of years as we see in the Middle East. The ego has set up certain defenses that are designed to prevent you from getting to the point where you consciously acknowledge that a new idea requires you to re-evaluate your existing knowledge or your reaction to life. The ego will do anything it can to prevent you from thinking creatively, from being conscious of what you are doing and from making conscious, creative decisions. To that end, the ego has several weapons that are effective in terms of keeping people from thinking outside their existing mental boxes—the boxes designed by the ego and the power elite that dominated the society in which you grew up.

13 | BLACK-AND-WHITE THINKING AND THE EGO

One of the most formidable traps for the human mind – and one of the primary causes of evil – is what I would like to call black-and-white thinking. The name implies that this is a form of thinking that is focused on two extremes that are seen as complete opposites. Only the opposites exist, and there are no nuances between them and thus no possibility for reconciliation between them. The opposites can only be in conflict, and there are only two ways of resolving the conflict:

- One opposite submits to the other (which is highly unlikely given that they are opposites).

- One opposite destroys the other.

The most obvious examples of such black-and-white extremes are true and false, right and wrong, good and evil, God and the devil. The intellect is the primary faculty for analyzing and labeling information that comes to us. The intellect doesn't really think about the meaning of the information; it simply analyzes it based on the criteria that are defined in the categories of the subconscious database. The intellect cannot make the decision that a new piece of information requires your conscious mind to change your world view or modify or reject old patterns of behavior. The intellect functions much like a computer that mechanically organizes data without making moral or ethical judgments about its meaning.

The only way that a new piece of information can produce a change in your mind is that the intellect presents this information to the conscious mind. You can then make a conscious, creative decision concerning how to apply the new information.

What creates our current limitations is that we have a limited understanding of life. The only way to escape our current limitations is to expand our understanding by asking questions and finding new information. For every problem and every limitation we face, there is a specific idea that can help us overcome the limitation.

Our limitation is caused by our current understanding of life, our current mental box. The only way to overcome the limitation is to accept a new idea, but where is this idea going to come from? It will have to come from *outside* our current mental box! If the idea was *inside* our mental box, we would already have accepted it and have used it to free ourselves from the limitation. If our current approach to healing could tell us how to cure cancer, we would have already done so.

Everything depends on how the intellect deals with a new idea, an idea that is outside our current mental box. Does the intellect find criteria that allows it to readily file it away so that your conscious mind is not even aware of it? Or does the intellect find it necessary to present it to your conscious mind? Only ideas that are presented to the conscious mind have a chance of producing any change in your life. We can still choose to ignore or reject them, but at least we have to do so consciously instead of having the intellect simply file the ideas away.

Once again, this is a useful mechanism, but the potential problem is that the ego can take advantage of it and prevent our conscious minds from even noticing ideas that are outside our current mental box. Once we have accepted a certain mental box, the box becomes the criteria for evaluating information, meaning the intellect will filter out any information that challenges the mental box. The mental box has become a closed system, a catch-22.

How black-and-white thinking filters information

Black-and-white thinking goes beyond the intellect's normal procedure for processing information because it imposes a value judgment as the overriding criteria for evaluating information. Black-and-white thinking creates two main categories in the subconscious database. One is for information that is good, reliable, true, valid, constructive, etc. The other is for information that is bad, untrue, false, unreliable, dangerous or evil.

These two overall categories still have any number of file folders to organize the information. If a new idea is labeled by the intellect as being evil information, then the idea will be filed away without being presented to the conscious mind. This sets up a catch-22 that is even more subtle and thus more powerful than the emotional catch-22. Let us look at a few examples.

Let us go back to the time when most people in Europe believed the earth was flat. As a child, this was mind-boggling to me, but what was even more shocking was that it took decades before people abandoned the belief in a flat earth.

Even after Columbus came back from his voyages, many people refused to believe him. Those who had been brought up with the belief that the earth was flat refused to accept the reality that the earth is round. How could they refuse to accept reality? Because their belief system was based on Catholic doctrine, and thus anything that seemed to challenge the church's world view was labeled as dangerous, meaning people did not truly think about it. Church doctrine did not specifically state that the earth was flat, but it did state that the earth was the center of the universe, which was based on seeing the earth as a flat disc and the sky as a dome covering the disc. The belief that Catholic doctrine was infallible is the main reason many people resisted the reality that the earth is not the center of the universe, even causing the Catholic Church to persecute early scientists in order to suppress what we now know is the truth.

As a more contemporary example, take the conflict between Jews and Palestinians. How could this conflict possibly be overcome unless both sides were willing to examine their subconscious databases and look for something that unifies rather than divides them? As long as they look at each other based on a black-and-white value judgment, there can be no peace between them. As long as they look at each other through the filter of black-and-white thinking, the conflict will remain irreconcilable.

How black-and-white thinking masks contradictions

The fact that certain information is not presented to the conscious mind makes it possible for people to ignore or deny almost anything. One of the main causes of the collective insanity is that we human beings have such an incredible ability to deny what later will be seen as painfully obvious. It is as if our minds can have blinders that prevent us from seeing beyond certain boundaries, causing us to do things that are clearly self-destructive—seen in retrospect.

Let us look at one of the most extreme examples. The Nazis in Germany used black-and-white thinking to label Jews as the scapegoat, as the cause of all of Germany's problems. There was an irreconcilable conflict between the German people and the Jews. There was no way that the Jews could modify their behavior to change the situation because the Germans were so stuck in black-and-white thinking that they could see only one possible solution—the *Final Solution*.

When you have defined two black-and-white opposites, the conflict can be resolved in only one way, namely by one side of the conflict suppressing or destroying the other. To the Nazis, it seemed perfectly rational – based on intellectual analysis colored by an absolutist value judgment – to solve the problem by exterminating all Jews in Europe. We may think that the Nazis were bad or evil people, but if we do, it only shows that we are the victims of black-and-white thinking colored by a value judgment. The amazing fact is that although the top Nazi leaders were clearly more extreme than normal people, the lower-level German leaders were no different from most other people.

As mentioned, the commandant of Auschwitz was a devoted family man. During the day, he would oversee the extermination of Jewish children in the gas chambers, but after office hours he would come home and play with his own children who lived in a Bungalow inside the camp. How could he fail to see the glaring contradiction in his life? Because to him there was no contradiction. If you had asked him whether he thought it was wrong to kill children, he would most likely have answered "Yes, of course." The simple – yet also frightening – explanation is black-and-white thinking.

He had created a category in his subconscious database for the Jews, and they were labeled as being not human. He could exterminate the Jews without feeling any moral scruples because he did not truly think he was killing human beings like his own children. His acceptance of this black-and-white view was so absolute that any challenging thought most likely never reached his conscious mind. It was filed away by his subconscious mind in the database created by his intellect—the intellect that cannot make moral or ethical judgments because it cannot decide which argument is more convincing than another.

"How is this possible," you might ask, and the answer is what we said about computers. You can search the Internet and find any number of websites whose content you will find highly offensive. They might contain child pornography, incite hatred, encourage Jihad or deny that the Holocaust ever took place. To the server on which those web pages are stored, there is nothing offensive at all.

To the intellect, nothing is offensive or wrong either. Once your conscious mind has created a category in your database and set up the parameters for what information should be stored there, the intellect will file away any new information that meets the criteria without presenting it to your conscious mind. It will even pull out a response to certain situations based on previous responses stored in the database—allowing you to respond to a situation without consciously or creatively thinking about it.

It is your conscious mind that decides to impose a value judgment and create the "Good" and "Evil" categories in the subconscious database. Once these categories have been set up, the intellect will not challenge them. The intellect does not understand what you mean with good and evil; it simply sorts information based on the criteria you have defined, meaning the intellect will never challenge your black-and-white world view. If you define information that validates Catholic doctrine as "good" and any contrary information as "evil," the intellect will never challenge your definition. This creates a catch-22, and it will persist until your conscious mind decides to begin consciously acknowledging new information and seeing where you have contradictions in your world view. Your intellect will never see such contradictions.

How black-and-white thinking creates conflict

In order to fully understand how black-and-white thinking creates irreconcilable conflicts, we need to dig deeper. Black-and-white thinking allows us to ignore information that challenges our mental box. It does not allow us to ignore that such information exists in the world and that it is a threat, either to our mental box, to our thought system or to some overall goal, such as the establishment of God's kingdom or the perfect political system. Black-and-white thinking allows us to think that we do not have to change *our own* minds, but it also emphasizes the need for other people to change *their* minds. This can be understood by taking a closer look at the very nature of black-and-white thinking.

The foundation for black-and-white thinking is the concept that the sphere of knowledge and ideas can easily be divided into two categories: true and false, constructive and dangerous, good and evil. This leads to the assumption that there is only one truth, and therefore any ideas that contradict or even go beyond that one truth must be false, dangerous or evil. Instead of dealing with neutral information, we have now imposed a value judgment on top of the process whereby we evaluate information. This inevitably sets up a conflict between the two types of information—or rather the people who believe in them. There is no way that the two types of information can be reconciled or can peacefully co-exist. There is an inherent conflict, and the only possible outcome is that one type of information wins by eradicating the other type.

What really turns this into a conflict-producing machine is the addition of thought systems. Again, there is nothing inherently problematic about creating a thought system. What has raised us above former limitations is our inherent curiosity. We have a real need to understand the world in which we live, and since the world is complex, it is natural to seek to organize our knowledge into a coherent system.

The creation of different systems does not necessarily create conflict. One of the major sources of human conflict is religion, but most of the world's mainstream religions have what is often called a mystical branch. In the mystical world view, God is beyond words and concepts, even beyond form. The goal of the mystic is union with God, which requires us to go beyond form. There is no religion that can define God, as the formless cannot be defined by or confined to any form. A religion can never have a monopoly on God and be the exclusive way to enter God's kingdom. Any religion is simply a signpost, a way-shower. It points you towards the goal, but there could be more than one valid way to get there. To the mystical world view, there is no inherent conflict between religions, but that is because true mystics have gone beyond black-and-white thinking.

When you take any thought system and approach it through the filter of black-and-white thinking, the inevitable consequence is that the system becomes exclusivist. It presents itself as the only system that contains true and valid information. This inevitably creates a distinction because it means that any information that contradicts or goes beyond the only true system is per definition false. This sets up an inevitable and irreconcilable conflict between all exclusivist belief systems. This explains why such systems become closed systems, closed mental boxes, that it can be very difficult to escape. The system sets up the two categories of good and evil in the subconscious database. Once they are established, any idea that goes beyond or challenges the system is automatically rejected as evil. That is precisely why it took so long for people to let go of the ideas that the earth is flat or that it is the center of the universe.

A religion is particularly vulnerable to this mechanism because it deals with God, which is defined as the ultimate authority or truth. A substantial portion of historical conflicts have involved religion. What really happens here is a very subtle mechanism. If we look at the core of the concept of God, we will see that God must by nature be non-local. If God is the source of all creation, if God is the ultimate reality, then God must be undivided, even indivisible—meaning that God is truly the only non-local reality that exists.

The claim that there is only one true religion and that this religion is the only way to know God or enter his kingdom is not non-local. It is highly localized because it is based on the division between God and that which is not God or is outside of God. What black-and-white thinking does to religion is to turn God into a localized concept, meaning that now there is an opposite to God, often called the devil. How can a truly non-local reality have an opposite?

There could be ways to approach truth that are non-local and thus do not create conflict. Once we allow black-and-white thinking to color our approach to truth, then conflict is inevitable. The reason is that all conflict springs from the illusion of locality—and black-and-white thinking is a direct offspring of this illusion. There is simply no way to overcome human conflict unless we go beyond black-and-white thinking.

Materialism and black-and-white thinking

In recent years several prominent materialists have written books that label religion as the cause of all human conflict. They argue that humankind faces the choice of either destroying ourselves or abandoning religion in favor of a strictly materialistic thought system. I understand that many people are concerned about religious conflict, as I have been since childhood. What these materialists have overlooked is that it is not religion itself that causes conflict—it is a black-and-white approach to religion.

Black-and-white thinking is not confined to the area of religion. When it is applied to political ideologies, we also see the creation of exclusivist thought systems that are in irreconcilable conflict with competing ideologies. A classical example is communism versus capitalism or Nazism versus anything else. When black-and-white thinking is applied to science, we see the creation of another exclusivist thought system, namely materialism. The very claim that materialism has a monopoly on truth and is the only way to secure a golden future is simply another example of black-and-white thinking. The efforts to eradicate religion will not *decrease* the amount of tension and conflict in the world—it will only *increase* it.

We could reason that all existing thought systems are polluted by black-and-white thinking and thus unable to secure peace. We could say that we need to formulate a new thought system and then go out and promote it as the only true way to peace. We need to replace all the faulty thought systems with our perfect one.

The ego would love nothing more than to see us do that. Another option is to seek an even deeper understanding of how the ego works so we can truly get to the bottom of the cause of evil.

The end can justify the means

What causes black-and-white thinking to spawn conflict is that it defines a supreme cause. For example, a religion may say that the supreme cause is to establish God's kingdom on earth or to save all people by bringing them into a celestial kingdom. In order to fulfill this goal, it is necessary that all people be converted to the one true religion. A political ideology may define the supreme goal as the establishment of a completely just economic system. It is necessary to convert all nations to a Marxist or communist ideology—or to forcefully subdue or eliminate those who will not be converted. Scientific materialism defines the supreme goal as getting all people to abandon religious superstition and accept the truth that can only be known through science.

For the umpteenth time, establishing a goal is not dangerous in itself. How do we produce progress without some kind of goal to work towards? The problem is that black-and-white thinking creates a supreme goal of epic importance, meaning that it can override any and all other concerns. This goal defines both a stick and a carrot, namely the promise of ultimate reward and the threat of ultimate punishment. If all people are converted to fundamentalist Christianity, all people will live forever in Paradise, and if not they will suffer forever in a fiery hell. The effect is that it becomes of supreme importance to reap the reward and avoid the punishment. This leads to a subtle psychological mechanism that has created more suffering and produced more atrocities than anything else in this world.

The mechanism is based on a very subtle idea, namely that the need to reach the supreme goal can justify any means available—even means that would normally be considered unacceptable. The Crusades saw Muslims killing Christians and Christians killing Muslims. Both sides claimed to believe in the same God and believed that they were actually killing other people in order to further God's supreme goal of saving humankind. The interesting thing is that both sides also honored the Old Testament in which we find a distinctly non-local command: "Thou shallt not kill!" I know full well that the Old Testament has other sections in which God supposedly commanded his chosen people to kill their enemies. Yet the command not to kill is truly unconditional. It does not define any – localized – conditions according to which killing becomes acceptable. It is a non-local command. Never under any circumstances kill another human being! How do we explain that two groups of people could believe that they were doing God's work by violating God's command not to kill?

As I argued earlier, Jesus' original teachings were non-local. Although there are some exceptions, the basic teachings of the Koran are likewise non-local. What actually happened was that some people who were trapped in black-and-white thinking turned the original non-local teachings into two localized, exclusivist thought systems. The two systems shared a common heritage, and they even defined the same goal, namely the salvation of humankind. The problem was that each of them – because they were based on black-and-white thinking – defined itself as the only means for reaching that goal.

To each religion it became of supreme importance to convert all people to its own system. The original goal of saving all people became secondary or identical to the goal of making all people followers of the one true religion. It followed that those who would not be voluntarily converted were not only a threat to God's overall plan but were destined to go to hell for eternity. It suddenly seemed as if killing these people would actually secure the fulfillment of God's overall plan and even prevent the people from going to hell.

I am not trying to argue that this is logical. I am simply pointing out that what we have here is the creation of a distinct mindset, namely the belief that the supreme end can justify any means. This mindset can "justify" even the most extreme human atrocities. Once we have defined the supreme goal of purifying the human race, killing six million people in concentration camps is not seen as wrong; it is seen as a perfectly justifiable means for reaching the goal. When seen through the filter of black-and-white thinking, it seems perfectly logical.

The Christian crusaders believed their God had commanded them not to kill. They believed Jesus had commanded them to not resist evil and to turn the other cheek. Yet they used black-and-white thinking to impose a value judgment according to which Muslims were so evil and such a threat to God's plan that it was not wrong to kill them. This created a new category in the subconscious database, and it now made conditional the unconditional command not to kill.

When the mind of a crusader received the input that he had killed another human being, the intellect would perform a neutral evaluation of that information: "Was the person a Muslim?" If the answer was "no," the intellect would have presented the information to the conscious mind that what the person had just done seemed to contradict the command not to kill. If the answer was "yes," the information was simply filed away as an acceptable event that required no conscious or creative evaluation.

Right here we can explain why human beings have committed such unbelievable atrocities against others and even destroyed themselves. It all boils down to how the ego has used black-and-white thinking to impose value judgments that control – localize – the way our minds process information. This can make us absolutely blind to the consequences of our actions and the need to change.

When will your life change? Your intellect will not change it, only your conscious mind can do so. If a new idea is not presented to the conscious mind because it is labeled as dangerous, how can there be change? People will keep doing the same thing, which is why the collective insanity called conflict, violence and war has been going on for so long. When will status quo change? When a critical mass of people make a conscious, creative decision to raise themselves above black-and-white thinking and then go out and expose it for others to see.

14 | THE OPPOSITE OF BLACK-AND-WHITE THINKING

How do we begin to raise ourselves out of the mental box created by black-and-white thinking? There are two basic ways:

- The School of Hard Knocks.

- The School of Increased Awareness.

Some societies have been in the School of Hard Knocks for centuries, even millennia. In some areas there used to be a lot of fighting, such as Europe, but people seem to have started to move away from conflict. Imagine how much more progress could be made if more people around the world became aware of the effects of black-and-white thinking and decided to consciously enroll in the School of Increased Awareness.

There is an interesting insight about the School of Hard Knocks that might help facilitate this shift in awareness. When you step back and look at the big picture, you become aware of the need to ask a question:

"Do people in the School of Hard Knocks create the knocks themselves?"

From a superficial viewpoint, it might seem like the religions of the world are very different. Yet virtually all of them contain some variant of one particular principle, namely what in Christianity is expressed this way: "Do onto others as you want them to do onto you." We can express this principle in a slightly different way: The universe is a mirror.

Virtually all of the religions of the world have been telling us that there is an advantage – to ourselves – by treating other people like we would like to be treated. Is it possible that these religions are based on an observation of a general life principle, a law of nature (as science likes to call it)? Is it possible that this insight is that the universe is somehow set up to reflect back to us what we are sending out? The way we treat others will determine what the cosmic mirror is sending back to us.

If the universe really is designed to act like a mirror, it has some profound implications. A mirror can only reflect back what is sent into it. Imagine that you come across a person who is sitting in front of a mirror with a frown on her face. You walk up to her and ask what she is doing. Here is her reply: "I am trying to get the image in the mirror to smile at me, but it just won't do it."

In a flash you realize that this person has completely failed to understand the natural law for how a mirror works. It is obvious that if you want your mirror image to smile at you, you have to first smile at the mirror. If you keep frowning at the mirror and expect that the mirror image will smile back at you, you are insane. Consider how many people on this planet would like their circumstances to change. Yet they nevertheless keep approaching life with the exact same attitude and mindset. Compare the saying that the universe is a mirror to Einstein's statement: "If you keep doing the same thing and expect a different result, you are insane." What has brought humankind to where we are today is our willingness to ask questions beyond our existing mental box. We can now formulate this in a different way. What has truly changed our lives is that some people have been willing to stop doing the same old thing. They have been willing to start by changing themselves, meaning that they were willing to question their mental box, their paradigm, their world view, their beliefs or whatever you want to call it. This points to a general principle: If you want your life to change, start by changing yourself. If you want your *outer* circumstances to change, start by changing your *inner* circumstances.

The School of Hard Knocks is created by people's mindset. It is your state of consciousness that creates the hard knocks, and the knocks will only get harder until you change your consciousness. The only question is how hard the knocks will have to get before you wake up, decide that you have had enough and then start looking for a better way.

If you go into black-and-white thinking, it is almost inevitable that you will attract to you another group of people who are likewise trapped in this form of thinking. *Your* absolute truth will then be in conflict with *their* absolute truth. You both get back what you are projecting out, and you are delivering the return for each other.

If you don't believe me, just take a little vacation in Jerusalem and talk to some Jews and Palestinians. I have already mentioned how the two sides have created categories in their subconscious databases and that this has led to a negative spiral. The consequence of such a spiral is that the knocks continue to get harder. An action from one side will release a far greater response today than it did last year or ten years ago. In the spring of 2009, the Palestinian Hamas sent a number of home-made rockets into Israel and killed one Israeli. The

Israelis sent the army into the Gaza Strip, and killed 1,500 Palestinians, a substantial portion of them women and children. The next blow is going to be even harder, and this will continue until a shift occurs, namely that one side decides to do what all religions tell us to do, namely to respond to violence with non-violence.

From a wider perspective, bot Israelis and Palestinians are saying to life that they want an opponent, they want a scapegoat they can blame for their problems. The Jews are simply giving the Palestinians what they want, and vice versa. So why do they hate each other so much? They should really be thanking each other for providing the life experience both sides want.

The second law and the School of Hard Knocks

Is there any indication from the field of science that supports the claim that the universe is a mirror and that we create the knocks in the School of Hard Knocks? Physicists have discovered a truly fundamental law, a law that governs everything that happens in the material universe. It is called the law of action and reaction. It states that for every *action,* there will be an opposite *reaction* of equal strength. The harder we knock, the harder the reactive knock will be. The strength of our action determines the strength of the reaction.

There is another law that is equally fundamental but more descriptive. It is called the second law of thermodynamics, and it says that in a closed system, disorder will increase until the system has reached the lowest possible energy state, meaning that all structures have been broken down.

What the second law really says is that when any system becomes closed, an internal resistance will cause ordered and organized structures to break down until there are no structures left. Any closed system will inevitably self-destruct. This is a parallel to the idea that the universe is a mirror and that if we take on a certain mindset, we will attract an opponent with the same mindset. We will create conflicts that will get progressively worse until we destroy each other.

The mindset created through black-and-white thinking is an example of a closed system. This form of thinking leads to the creation of thought systems that each claim to be the ultimate and superior system. Precisely because these thought systems claim exclusivity, they inevitably become closed. If you have the ultimate and superior truth, why would you need to learn anything from any source outside your system? When we create such systems, we close ourselves off from the world, and we inevitably set up a clash between our own closed system and any other closed system out there. If you look at history, you see that these closed systems don't appear one at a time. There seems to always be at least two, and that is why there will inevitably be a clash between them.

The real cause of conflict

The vast majority of human conflicts and wars have involved such closed thought systems. As we see in the field of religion, conflicts between closed thought systems can go on for centuries, even millennia. The conflicts tend to get worse until the resulting violence finally becomes so unbearable that at least some people start wondering if there is a better way.

The way out of such conflicts is that people either abandon the closed systems or turn the systems into more open ones that can indeed coexist with other thought systems. The medieval Catholic Church is the textbook example of a closed thought system that sought to defend its superior, exclusive position with all means available. When enough people refused to allow their minds to be confined to the mental box created by the system, the system could not suppress all of them. Eventually the system faced the choice to either open up or die. The underlying cause of the collective insanity is that our minds have a tendency to create closed "systems" or even closed mind states. Once created, they become self-perpetuating negative spirals that will inevitably end in disaster.

The human psyche contains two tendencies. One is the love and curiosity that drives progress, and it is obvious that love and curiosity can never be closed. The other tendency is fear, and it is obvious that fear does cause us to close off our minds. Out of fear we seek to create the perfect system that can withstand all challenges, and numerous people throughout history have believed in – and sacrificed their lives for – the dream of creating the perfect system that can never break down. The attempt to create such a closed system is directly against the most fundamental laws of physics. It would be foolhardy and arrogant to think that we human beings can work against the basic forces of the universe. Nevertheless, that has not stopped people from trying, and even today you see people – in the field of religion, in the field of politics and even in the field of science – who are trying to create the perfect system.

Is it possible that there never can be a perfect system of thought? Is it possible that the perfect "system" is to maintain our curiosity and continually look for a higher understanding of life?

The opposite polarity to black-and-white

What happens when people have had enough of the hard knocks and finally see the futility of the endless conflicts between thought systems that each claim to have the one, absolute truth? What often happens is that people become open to a very simple idea that can be expressed this way: "All religions in the world claim that their God is the one true God and that their way to God is the only true way. Obviously, those claims cannot all be right – there cannot be more than one true God – so what if all of them are wrong?"

This is an important question, and it can help people escape the mental box created by black-and-white thinking. However, there is a real risk that people will instead end up in a new mental box, namely the one created by the opposite polarity to black-and-white thinking. Escaping black-and-white thinking doesn't mean you are home free.

In order to explain this, we need to examine the underlying assumption that generates black-and-white thinking. Let take another look at the difference between locality and non-locality. Non-locality is oneness, a state in which there are no divisions or irreconcilable differences. It follows that locality is the opposite, namely a state in which there are – or seems to be – divisions and irreconcilable differences. How do divisions occur? Division as a concept implies that you take a unified whole and then divide it into at least two compartments. What sets these two parts apart from the whole and from each other is their differences. Locality implies the establishment of two opposite polarities that are then used to define differences between the divisions of the whole. In its extreme form, this leads to the creation of two opposites that are opposites in every way, such as black and white, right and wrong, good and evil.

The creation of division leads to a world view, a form of thinking, that we might call dualistic thinking. The basic concept is that reality truly is divided into two opposites and thus everything must be defined based on the differences between these opposites. Nothing is neutral because everything must be put on a scale. The scale has two extremes, such as good and evil, and in the middle is a sort of neutral point between the two extremes. Everything in life must be evaluated in relation to where it fits on this scale. Everything is either good, evil or somewhere in between because there is nothing outside the dualistic scale.

We now need to step back and realize that contrary to first appearances, black-and-white thinking is actually a form of *relative* thinking. The reason is that it evaluates everything based on how it fits on the scale with two extremes. Everything is evaluated based on its position *relative* to the two extremes. There is nothing absolute in this form of thinking because something absolute can only be found outside the scale—the scale upon which everything is relative to the two extremes. The confusing thing is that black-and-white thinking causes people to make the claim that their system has an absolute truth. This claim is an illusion.

Mysticism sees God as the ultimate non-local reality because God is beyond all form. We cannot create an image or concept in this world that accurately describes God. Any image or concept has form, and form can never describe the formless.

In contrast to the mystical view, most mainstream religions have been turned into black-and-white thought systems. This can happen only because people have come to accept a dualistic world view. In this world view, it is possible to divide reality into two spheres, one in which God resides and one in which God is not found.

Dualistic thinking cannot fathom the formless, non-local nature of God. Duality turns God into something that has form, but as soon as you clothe God in form, it follows inevitably that the God of form must have an opposite. You can now create a relative scale with God at one end and the devil or hell at the other end. The problem here is that the formless has been lost in the process. When you step into dualistic thinking, you are no longer dealing with the formless God but a graven image. You have made God in your own – localized – image and likeness.

Black-and-white thinking is really an offspring of dualistic thinking, the form of thinking that divides reality by creating a relative scale with an opposite polarity at either end. Black-and-white thinking is not the only possible outcome of dualistic thinking—it is simply one extreme. In duality, everything has an opposite so black-and-white thinking also has an opposite, namely what I like to call "gray thinking."

Black-and-white thinking is based on a very simple concept, namely that the two polarities defined by the dualistic world view should also become the subject of a value judgment, meaning one polarity is "good" and the other "evil." It is precisely this value judgment that sets up irreconcilable conflicts between God and the devil, between two religions, between capitalism and communism and any other set of opposites. When a value judgment is applied, the two opposites can only be in conflict and the only possible outcome is that one opposite destroys the other.

Of course, the two opposites could not actually exist without each other, as action cannot exist without reaction. It is impossible that relative good could destroy relative evil. Spending one's life seeking to create the perfect system that will secure the triumph of good over evil is an impossible and entirely futile task. One relative polarity can never destroy its own opposite—they can only exist as a pair because that is the only way to divide unity into separate compartments.

Black-and-white thinking creates the School of Hard Knocks, and as the knocks become hard enough, some people begin to awaken. They begin to see the fallacy of black-and-white thinking, especially its value judgment that can only create conflict. It is now quite likely that such people will come to focus on the problem of value judgment and reason that what truly creates conflict is the tendency to judge based on this black-and-white scale with two extremes.

They reason that the way to overcome conflict is to avoid the value judgment. In order to do this, they still have to find a way to deal with the relative scale with two extremes. The most common way of doing this is to ignore or deny the two extremes, adopting a world view that is focused on the center portion of the relative scale instead of the end points. Black-and-white thinking focuses on the end points whereas gray thinking is focused in the middle, gray being the mixture of black and white.

Gray thinking does not lead to true peace

We now need to make a subtle distinction. The majority of conflicts on earth are the outcome of black-and-white thinking. If all people moved from black-and-white thinking into gray thinking, the world would indeed become a more peaceful place. However, this would not actually help us awaken from the collective insanity.

The insanity is not caused by black-and-white thinking; it is caused by something deeper, namely dualistic, relative thinking. Black-and-white thinking is only one outcome of this form of thinking, and gray thinking is the opposite polarity to it. We do not awaken from the common insanity by moving from one outcome of dualistic thinking into the other outcome of the same form of thinking. The only real way to awaken from the collective insanity is to step completely outside of dualistic thinking by stepping away from the relative scale, the scale with two extremes. It is this scale that gives rise to the illusion of separation and locality. In order to awaken from the insanity, we have to free our minds from these illusions so we can connect to the underlying, non-local reality.

Many people are firmly convinced that black-and-white thinking gives them a true, real and accurate view of reality. Many of them are truly well-meaning people who believe they are working to bring peace to earth. Their vision for how this can happen is that their thought system is elevated to a status of exclusivity by eradicating all competing thought systems (and possibly the people who follow them). Obviously, this is an impossible dream, but until people see that, they will have to stay in the School of Hard Knocks. This means true peace will not come about as a result of the people trapped in black-and-white thinking.

The only people who have a realistic potential for bringing peace are those who have moved out of black-and-white thinking. The problem is that too many of them have become trapped in gray thinking. Why is that a problem, since gray thinking makes people more peaceful? The problem is that gray thinking only makes people more peaceful in the sense that it pacifies them. They tend to think that since nothing is really true or false, good or evil, nothing is really worth fighting for, nothing really matters.

The consequence is that nothing is really worth working for, especially if it means challenging the aggressive people who are stuck in black-and-white thinking. If we don't challenge these people, they will – precisely because they are aggressive and think something is worth fighting for – take over our society and public debate. That means our public debate will be based on black-and-white thinking with no consideration for any alternatives. If our debate does not deal with the fallacies of black-and-white thinking, how will we ever move out of this form of thinking and the conflict it spawns?

The realistic answer is that we will not move away from conflict. Instead, humankind will continue to pursue the impossible dream of creating the ultimate thought system that will destroy all others. Many well-meaning people have seen the fallacy of religious thought systems only to come to believe that the way to peace is to create a materialistic thought system and then have it destroy all religions.

How black-and-white is like gray thinking

From a superficial viewpoint, it would seem that black-and-white thinking is the opposite of gray thinking. When we look deeper, we discover that they have similar effects on people's mindset. Both types of thinking form closed mental boxes because they make people believe that they know everything they need to know. Both forms of thinking tend to shut off people's curiosity, which stops progress and traps people in a certain mental box. They both produce the same result, they simply do it in different ways.

It is easy to see that black-and-white thinking has a strong appeal to the emotions. This form of thinking mainly gives rise to the emotions of fear and anger. The primary effect of fear, as we have seen, is that it paralyzes you. People trapped in black-and-white thinking may not appear to be paralyzed, because they can be very active in combating competing thought systems. They are paralyzed in the sense that they cannot question or look beyond their own thought system.

A classical example is how medieval Catholics were afraid to question Catholic doctrine out of fear of either hell or the Inquisition. Even in today's world, many people take a fundamentalist approach to their religion and are afraid to question it. Once people have accepted a thought system, it forms a closed mental box that they cannot get out of. Many people are so afraid of considering any idea that is beyond their thought system that they have effectively killed their imagination and curiosity. They often believe that their thought system is the only reliable source of truth and that it tells them everything they are allowed to know. Their fear literally forms an emotional prison that keeps them trapped.

Once you escape the paralyzing effect of this kind of fear, the fear of religious people can seem completely irrational, even ridiculous. Many people who are trapped in gray thinking feel they have risen above emotions and are rational, logical and intelligent people. Gray thinking also has a very strong emotional appeal, only it gives rise to a different form of emotion. The primary emotion produced by gray thinking is pride. Whereas fear and anger are obvious emotions, pride is a very subtle emotion that is often not recognized by the people who have it. Many intellectual people have a subtle sense of being superior to those who do not share their intellectual world view. Pride is just as effective as fear in forming a closed mental box. Once people have accepted a thought system that appeals to the intellect – such as scientific materialism – they will believe it is the only reliable source of truth. They may not be afraid to look beyond or question their thought system, but since they are firmly convinced that it is superior, they see no reason for doing so.

I have already described how this attitude caused 19th century scientists to believe they had made all the major discoveries, and this shows the major limitation of pride. It makes people feel there could not possibly be anything to discover beyond the boundaries defined by their thought system. This kills curiosity as effectively as fear. Many intellectual people look down upon religious people while failing to realize that their attitude and their thought system is as much of a hindrance to progress as is religion. It is dangerous to put limitations on where science might take us in the future. True science is an open-ended process, and saying that science will never prove the existence of anything beyond the material universe is either incredibly arrogant or incredibly unintelligent.

Black-and-white and gray thinking spring from the same basic illusion, namely duality. They also have the same basic effect, namely to close our minds to new ideas. Regardless of the fact that many intellectual people think they contribute more to peace than religious people, the reality is that both forms of thinking only serve to maintain the collective insanity by allowing the ego to hide.

The ego's main objective is to keep you under its control. Whether this happens through fear or through pride makes no never-mind to the ego. Nor does it make any difference to the ruling power elite whether they have to appeal to people's fears or their pride. A smart power elite will gladly let certain people feel superior as long as they can stay in control behind the scenes. Whether you are too afraid to look or too proud to look, the act of not looking outside your current mental box is precisely what perpetuates the collective insanity.

What can change the equation? Only that a sufficient number of people realize the need to move away from both black-and-white and gray thinking and completely transcend dualistic thinking with its relative scale. We must strive for a different way to approach reality, one that is not based on separation, division and locality. In order to do that, we need to understand the most subtle effect of both black-and-white and gray thinking, namely that they create mind states that become the perfect traps for our minds because we never question the perception upon which they are based.

15 | THE CREATION OF MIND STATES

We will now examine the most subtle – and thus the most seductive – effect of the ego. In order to be free of this effect, we have to be willing to take a critical look at our lives and question something that the vast majority of people never even dream of questioning. That something is our perception of life.

Is the way you perceive life really the way life is? Or is it possible that the way you perceive life is just that— one among many ways to perceive life? Is it possible that all of the ways that people perceive life are out of touch with – and thus give distorted views of – the way life truly is? Is it possible that all human beings are trapped in a polluted perception that makes us think we see reality, but what we see is a distorted image? As long as we are trying to solve our problems through that distorted perception, we have no chance whatso-ever of escaping evil. Instead, we will remained trapped by evil while being ignorant of this fact.

Normally, when we use the word ignorance, we mean that there is something we do not know. There was a time when no one knew about the health risk of smoking. People were innocently ignorant about the dangers of smoking. Today, everyone knows about the dangers of smoking, but some people smoke anyway. How can we explain this? We can explain it by defining a new type of ignorance.

The worst possible form of ignorance is not that we know nothing. It is that we do know something, but what we know is not accurate or complete—*yet we think it is*. The worst possible form of ignorance is that we look at life through polluted or incomplete perception, but we think what we see is not an image but reality itself. It is comparable to a person who is wearing yellow glasses, yet he is firmly convinced that what he sees through the glasses is not colored in any way but is the way things really look. He is convinced that the sky really is green and that there is nothing wrong with his perception.

Perception is not a passive process

We have all been brought up with a very limited understanding of perception. For example, when I say the word "perception" most people will link it to the senses. Perception is seeing or hearing. In reality, the eyes do not perceive; the eyes simply detect light waves, turn them into a kind of digital signal and then send that signal to the brain.

Perception is performed by the mind. The intellect takes the raw signals from the eyes and imposes patterns upon them, turning them into data. Then the intellect uses the categories in the subconscious database to analyze and categorize the data. Some of it is filed away, some of it is used to – still subconsciously – select a response and some of it is presented to the conscious mind. The ultimate outcome of perception is that sensory data is turned into information. It is only the *conscious* mind that can turn data into information. It is only the conscious mind that can use that information to question its perception or revise its basic view of life. This leads us to another common misunderstanding about perception.

Most of us were taught that perception is a passive process. Your eyes register the light waves that are received from the outside. This is true as far as the eyes are concerned, but as we have seen, it is not true for the mind.

The mind is not passively receiving signals. The mind is actively imposing patterns upon the sensory signals and then analyzing and organizing them. Much of this happens below the level of conscious awareness, but once data is turned into information, the conscious mind can deal with that information in a variety of ways. It might label a piece of information as dangerous, it might decide to ignore it or it might decide to use it to revise its entire world view.

None of these actions are passive—they are all highly active. They are not what we traditionally call perception, but that is because of our limited understanding of perception. In reality, perception is a very active process that first creates information and then does something with that information based on a set of very complicated criteria that are highly individual.

If we are to ever find a better way to deal with human evil, we have to find a way around the greatest obstacle to resolving conflict, namely that two individuals or two groups of people can look at the same situation but perceive it in entirely difference ways. The perceptions may be so different that people cannot even communicate.

Let us look at some examples. You have probably heard the classical example of an accident where five eyewitnesses give five different versions of the same event. We now see a very simple explanation. The eyes of each of the five people registered the same light waves, but the mind of each person

imposed different patterns on the input. The intellect of each
person then used its individual database to analyze the sensory
input, and as a result it selected certain aspects of the input
while ignoring others. Even though the *eyes* of all five people
saw the same thing, the *conscious minds* of the people were not
presented with the same data. On top of that, the conscious
minds then treated the data they did receive in different ways.

It now becomes obvious why the five people have different descriptions of the same event: They literally perceived the
event differently because of how their minds manipulated the
raw sensory input. Their minds took the same sensory input
but used it to produce different information, which is why the
people present different information to the investigator. Each
person claims: "This is what I saw," or even: "This is what
happened." The reality is that while each person is convinced
that his or her version is in accordance with what really happened, none of them may have an accurate perception of the
event.

As another example, take a divorce. Two people fell in love
and started living together because they felt they had so much
in common. The feeling of having something in common was
likely due to the fact that they looked at life in much the same
way—or so they thought. They started the relationship thinking they will always look at life the same way, but no sooner is
the honeymoon over than they start realizing that they do not
always perceive the same event the same way. They may struggle to cope with this for a while, but finally decide to divorce.
No sooner is the decision made than they find themselves
unable to communicate about anything. It is as if something
has happened to their perception so they no longer see the
same thing or reach the same conclusion.

One explanation is that the ego of each person has imposed
a filter on that person's perception, and thus all information

that relates to the spouse is colored with an overlay. If you have made the decision that another person is wrong or has wronged you, then everything that person does or says will be perceived through a filter. Because you do not want the other person to be right, nothing that person says will be perceived as right. If both people have such a filter, no real communication is possible.

Now take this to a broader level. The Jews and the Palestinians live together in the city of Jerusalem and one must assume that their eyes see the same thing. The experience of the Palestinians is starkly different from the experience of the Jews. Even the same event will be perceived very differently by the two sides. The only logical explanation is that the two sides each have a filter that completely colors how they perceive any event. There is a set of Jewish glasses and a set of Palestinian glasses.

If you could put on the Jewish glasses and then put on the Palestinian glasses, you would see the obvious differences. You would also see that both of the two sides are not seeing the reality of the situation but only a distorted image that is produced by their own subconscious minds. Neither of the two sides see this, and that is precisely why each side believes they are seeing reality and that it is the other side that has a biased, distorted and unrealistic view of the situation.

Each side is thinking that the only possible resolution is that the other sides adopts their own perception of the situation. None of the two sides is willing to consider that perhaps the only true resolution would be that both sides questioned their perception and did the hard work of clearing their perception so they could see reality instead of a colored image.

You may have heard the old saying: "Don't judge a man until you have walked in his moccasins for two weeks." We can now rewrite it as follows: "Don't think you understand a person until you have seen the world through his or her perception filter."

A quantum mechanical view of perception

Let me sketch a new approach to perception based on quantum physics. This branch of science distinguishes between two states:

- A physical event, such as the appearance of a subatomic particle.

- Before the physical event takes place, the particle does not exist as a particle. It exists as a *potential* particle. It is not in the physical realm but in what is called a quantum state or a state of potentiality.

Let us keep this simple by saying that a physicist makes an observation and perceives a subatomic particle. According to quantum physics, the particle was not there before the scientist made the observation. This does not mean that there was nothing there, but there was no physical "thing." Instead, there was a potential particle, an entity that existed in a different realm but had not yet been brought into the physical realm. The entity could manifest as different particles in different locations and with different properties. There may be ten potential outcomes, but when the physicist makes the observation, one potential is selected and now becomes a physical particle.

What is the scientist doing when she makes an observation? She is performing an act of perception, yet it is not a *passive* act of seeing something that is already there. It is an *active* process whereby the scientist's mind is interacting with the realm of probability and selecting one potential outcome that is then manifest as a physical particle. This shows that the mind of the scientist is not passive in the interaction. The mind is actively participating, and this must mean that perception is sending out something from the mind.

According to quantum physics, everything can be viewed as something called a "quantum waveform." Many scientists see this as an abstract entity, but when we compare this to the fact that everything is made from energy waves, we get a deeper explanation. Everything that exists is truly made from energy waves that are organized into a specific matrix. What gives this matrix its form? In our case our minds must have the ability to impose a thought form upon the energy waves and create a quantum waveform. Everything is a quantum waveform, so our minds are also quantum waveforms. This waveform is very complex, based on all of our past experiences, what I have called the contents of the subconscious database.

Let us now go back to the situation of five people viewing an accident. The accident itself took place in the macroscopic realm. There was a physical event, yet what the people saw was not the event itself. As a person observed the event, the person's mind sent a signal towards the event. That signal generated a return current in the form of visible light waves. As these signals came back to the person's mind, they now encountered the very complex quantum waveform that makes up the person's mind.

The energy signals coming back from the physical event are waves, and as they enter the person's mind, they begin to interact with the energy waves in the mind. Energy waves can reinforce or cancel out each other, and this is what happens when we perceive an event. Depending on the contents of our subconscious minds, some of the signals coming from the event can be canceled out and others can be magnified. Those that are canceled out will never reach the conscious mind. Those that are magnified will not only reach the conscious mind but will seem very important.

An accident may be an event towards which the spectators are fairly neutral, but now consider what happens when people view an event towards which they have strong feelings. If the subconscious database is strongly affected by black-and-white thinking, a person may not be neutral towards any aspect of life. The person may be constantly feeling threatened, and in an attempt to preserve some sense of being in control, the person's subconscious mind is sending out very powerful mental signals that can cancel out any threatening information before it even reaches the mind.

The person is not trying to see things as they really are; the person is using perception in an attempt to force the world to conform to how the person wants the world to be. The mind of such a person is permanently locked in a specific state that effectively prevents the person from ever seeing the world with neutral perception. The person's perception is polluted by a desire to make the world conform to a certain thought system created by human beings.

How perception creates mind states

I have earlier quoted Jesus and referred to science. I have always had the attitude that we need to seek useful ideas wherever they can be found. I would now like to quote the Buddha, specifically the opening verse in the main Buddhist scripture, The Dhammapada. There are a number of quite different translations of this verse, but to make it even more fun, I will give you a personal translation that is adapted to the vocabulary I have used in this book but true to the original meaning:

> Perception leads to the creation of mental states.
> To the mental state that is born from perception, perception is supreme and cannot be questioned.
> If you experience life through the filter of polluted perception, suffering follows you, as the wheel of the cart follows the foot of the ox that pulls it.

This verse was formulated 2,500 years ago, and it is an interesting demonstration of the fact that even though we think our civilization is so sophisticated, the basic understanding of human psychology has been available to us for a long time. During that time, few people have understood its deeper meaning, and the reason is that people have not had the understanding we have today. With the knowledge we have in our present civilization, we can uncover that meaning and also make it more practical and useful.

What the Buddha was saying is a confirmation of my claim that perception is an active process. Your basic attitude towards life, your thought system, your most subtle beliefs form a filter. That filter determines your perception, and it actively imposes a certain coloring on everything you experience. Because you do not "see" the glasses you are wearing, you think your way of perceiving life is the only way. Because you experience nothing that is not colored by the filter, you have no reference point of what the world looks like when not colored by the filter. You think the way you see life is the way life really is.

As you move through life, every situation you encounter, every person you meet, is colored by the filter of your perception. Your perception determines what aspect of the situation you focus on and what you ignore. As a basic example, an optimist will focus on the positive aspects of a situation while overlooking or downplaying the negative. A pessimist, naturally, will do the opposite. Is the glass half full or half empty?

When we compare this to the quantum mechanical model of perception, we gain an interesting perspective. Say an optimist and a pessimist are stranded on a deserted island. They both face ten potential outcomes of a the situation, ranging from very negative (you die) to very positive (you are rescued). Which one of the ten potential outcomes will become a reality?

Each person has the same potential outcomes so it is a matter of which one is selected. This selection process is an interaction between the realm of probability and the person's mind. Is it possible that the mind of the pessimist will select the worst possible outcome because the person's attitude forms a quantum waveform that cancels out the more positive outcomes? Likewise, the quantum waveform in the mind of the optimist will cancel out the negative outcomes. Again, we see that perception is far more than passively seeing something over which we have no influence.

The way you perceive life inevitably determines how you react to life. With "reaction" I mean not only actions, but more importantly your thoughts and feelings – your attitude – towards life. For example, if your perception is colored to focus on the negative aspects of life, your perception can generate a mind state in which you see yourself as a victim, thinking your life is controlled by forces beyond your control. You will therefore accept the belief that you are a dis-empowered being and that you have no power to change your destiny.

Your perception determines the way you react to life, and out of that reaction is born a specific psychological condition. The Buddha called it a "mental state," but because the word "mental" for most people refers to thought, I prefer to call it a "mind state." The reason is that a mind state clearly involves both what you think about life and what you feel about life.

Once your basic perception has created a mind state, your conscious mind can easily become trapped inside that mind state. You come to identify yourself with and as the mind state. You think you *are* the mind state and that there is nothing more to your identity.

Once you accept the mind state as your identity – and accept that the way life looks from inside the mind state is the way life really is – there is no way you can go back and question the basic perception that created the mind state in the first place. It is like the person who had yellow contact lenses mounted at birth and has never seen the sky without the glasses. How can this person question whether the sky really is green? How can the person question what it sees with its own eyes?

How mind states create perception

Take the optimist and the pessimist again. They might be experiencing the exact same situation, but the optimist focuses on the positive aspects of it and tends to overlook the negative. The person's basic perception of life is "colored" to emphasize the positive and filter out the negative. This perception then creates a mind state in which the person is generally happy and content with life. In contrast, the pessimist literally perceives life differently, focusing on the negatives while overlooking the positives. The mind state of a pessimist tends to become a downward spiral where the person gradually becomes more and more dissatisfied with life. This can lead to a state in which the person cannot enjoy anything in life, and it can even lead to more extreme states, such as depression, substance abuse or suicide. This isn't to say that the optimist's perception is better or more accurate. Many optimists tend to become passive and fail to change things in their lives that could easily be changed. Even optimists could benefit from questioning their perception of life and bring it into alignment with reality. Both forms of perception have the effect of causing us to ignore or deny certain aspects of life. This is not necessarily healthy and any form of denial contributes to the collective insanity. Optimists are not necessarily free from the insanity; many of them have simply adapted to it so they can live with it without turning negative. Is there a way to perceive life that is not colored by anything? If so, what might life look like when seen without any coloring?

Let us take a more emotionally charged example of mind states. Is it possible that identifying yourself as a "Jew" or a "Palestinian" is not an objective reality but a mind state? Each group of people have a basic, underlying perception of life. This perception has – over time – created a collective mind state for Jews and another for Palestinians—and numerous other mind states for different groups of people. When you are born into a group of people who identify themselves based on this mind state, you inevitably come to see life the same way. You build a mind state that is very much based on the collective state. Once you have accepted this mind state, you will be completely unable to see anything wrong with the perception that created the mind state.

If we try to step back from the emotions and take a neutral look at what it might take to create peace between Jews and Palestinians, we come to a simple realization: The Jews will never make peace with the Palestinians! It really is that simple. I know some intellectual people will think there must be some ultimate argument that can persuade both sides. I actually agree that there is such an argument, but it can only be

207 15 | The Creation of Mind States   207

found at a deeper level than both sides are seeing right now. When you experience the state of mind of both Jews and Palestinians, you realize that each group's frame of mind is based on a specific way of looking at their relationship—a specific form of perception. The simple reality is that the Jews do not "see" the situation the same way the Palestinians "see" it. This difference in perception is what has given rise to the state of mind – the attitude, the thoughts and feelings – of both sides. The way Jews and Palestinians see themselves in their current situation is not an objective reality but a specific mind states.

The Jews are in a mind state that is characterized by seeing themselves as persecuted people who have finally returned to the homeland given to them by God himself. In their absence, the Palestinians had moved in and now they refuse to acknowledge that the Jews have a superior and exclusive claim to the land. The Palestinians see themselves as oppressed people, first oppressed by the Ottoman Empire, then by the British and now by the Jews.

This sense of identity is not who these people really are—it is a mind state. Given that both Jews and Palestinians are in a mind state that is based on seeing themselves in opposition to other people, they can never make peace as long as they see the situation and their relationship from inside their respective mind state.

Is it possible that there could be peace between Jews and Palestinians and between some of the many other groups around the world that oppose each other based on a mind state? There is only one way this could come about: The people need to come to the realization that the reason there seems to be an irreconcilable conflict between them is that both are seeing their relationship from inside a certain mind state. If they are to ever change the situation, they have to stop doing the same thing while expecting a different result.

Each side has to stop demanding that the other side changes and comes to see the situation the same way they do. Each side has to be willing to step outside its own mind state and look at the situation without the coloring of that mind state. They have to stop seeing themselves and each other as Jews and Palestinians and start seeing each other as *human beings*. In order to step outside your mind state, you have to be willing to question the underlying perception that created the mind state.

Questioning your perception

I know it will seem like I am contradicting myself because I just said that once you have stepped into a certain mind state, you cannot question the perception that created the mind state. We can gain a deeper understanding by going back to how our minds process information.

A pessimist has created certain categories in his subconscious database and has defined criteria that cause his intellect to filter input in a specific way. Input that points to a positive aspect of life is filed away without being presented to the conscious mind. Input that points to a negative aspect is immediately presented to the conscious mind as proof that life really is messed up. Incidentally, many pessimists will, when their pessimistic outlook is challenged, make the following statement: "I'm not a pessimist; I'm a *realist!*" This proves that such people truly believe their pessimistic perception shows them life the way it really is.

This selective filtering of information is performed by the intellect, which is based on detecting differences. The intellect itself is not what creates the mind state. The mind state is created by the conscious mind based on a localized view of life. This localized view of life goes all the way back to the original perception. While the intellect does not create the mind state, it is impossible to escape the mind state by using the intellect. The reason is that the mind state is localized – defined by division based on differences – and the intellect is designed to analyze differences. Once the mind state is created by a combination of the localized view and the intellect, you cannot get out of the mind state by using the same mental processes that created it. As Einstein said, you cannot solve a problem with the same state of consciousness that led to the creation of the problem.

What can break the catch-22 is the realization that our minds have an intuitive faculty that is *not* designed to detect details and differences but is designed to see underlying connections and the big picture. By using the intuitive faculty to formulate and investigate some creative questions, we can begin to penetrate the veils in the mind—the veils that hide the underlying reality.

At present, Jews and Palestinians approach their relationship from the mind states that identify them as Jews or Palestinians. These mind states are based on a localized approach, and they are very much focused on differences. Hardly anyone thinks you can be a Jew and a Palestinian at the same time. You are either one or the other. The two groups have a conflict because of their differences, but those differences are tied to their mind states. When we go a step further, we have to question whether the differences are actually *created* by their mind states and thus could not exist independently of the mind states?

As long as the two groups look at the situation from inside their respective mind states, they can never make peace. They will always focus on their differences, and their subconscious minds will filter out any input that points toward similarities. They see only the differences and ignore their similarities. Are there similarities between Jews and Palestinians? Does a normal Jew have two arms, ten toes and one nose? Does a normal Palestinian have two arms, ten toes and one nose?" There are actually some similarities between them. Or as the old saying goes: "We all put our pants on the same way."

While people look at their relationship from inside their respective mind states, the similarities will be filtered out and the differences emphasized. If we step outside of the two mind states, we can begin to see an underlying unifying factor.

When we strip everything else away, Jews and Palestinians are both human beings. Plain and simple. From a purely biological viewpoint, they have far more similarities than differences. The differences exist mainly in the mind. Do they have any existence outside the mind? If they have no existence outside the mind, should they really be assigned such great importance?

If the differences could not exist independently of the mind, does that mean they are created by the mind? Are the differences we perceive between ourselves and others simply a product of our perception, a perception that is colored by the illusion of locality, division and separation? Is it possible that we have the ability to look beyond this illusion? Is it possible that if we do look beyond dualistic thinking, we will see an underlying reality that will empower us to awaken from the collective insanity that makes our personal lives miserable and creates seemingly irreconcilable conflicts between us?

Why we resist non-locality

At this point I know exactly what might be going on in your mind. Right now, there are two distinct voices talking inside your mind. One is the voice of hope that makes your heart swell and gives you a new sense that there might be a brighter future ahead. The other is a voice that is either screaming at you in panic – flashing a red sign that says "Danger, Danger" – or speaking to you very softly, reasoning why what I am saying here cannot possibly be right.

That second voice – be it loud or gentle – is the voice of the ego, and it is speaking to you because it has probably never felt more threatened than it does right now. The reason is that you are now on the threshold where you can take a decisive step away from being controlled by your ego. If you take this step, your ego will be exposed, and once exposed it can never have the same hold over you as before you started seeing the ego for what it is.

In a coming chapter we will consider some of the fundamental questions of life, namely: Who are you? Where did you – really – come from? Why are you here? Before we do this, we can benefit from considering why the ego does not want you to even consider these questions.

The ego wants you to continue to identify yourself based on the mind state into which it has so carefully manipulated you. It does not want you to question the mind state, but it especially does not want you to question the perception that created it. If you do question your perception, you will realize that you are not only more than your mind state, you are more than your perception. The "more" that you are can indeed perceive life the way it really is. Let us examine the very subtle mechanism that the ego uses to prevent us from discovering who we truly are.

16 | YOU ARE MORE THAN YOU THINK

Your present mind state gives you a sense of identity, a sense of who you are and how you fit into your society. This sense of identity is the result of programming you have received from without and your ego's influence from within. In order to survive, your ego must prevent you from realizing that you are more than this sense of identity. The ego does not want you to ask questions that might challenge your ego-created sense of identity. The ego will seek to accomplish this by making use of the mechanism described earlier.

Black-and-white thinking appeals to fear and gray thinking appeals to pride. Behind both forms of thinking is the underlying consciousness that you know everything there is to know—and thus you do not need to question your mind state or your perception. The underlying assumption is that what you already know – defined in your thought system and world view – is accurate, true, valid, complete, perhaps even infallible. Underneath both black-and-white and gray thinking is the need for security. This security requires that you, your thought system and your mind state must be right.

We have now uncovered the worst fear of the ego, namely the fear of being proven wrong. The ego has managed to manipulate you into a mind state that is based on a certain perception of life, including a particular thought system. The ego wants to keep you in that mental box, but what is one of the most powerful incentives for questioning your mental box? It is that something in your world view or thought system is proven wrong so definitively that your conscious mind cannot ignore it and thus has to revise its world view. The last thing the ego wants to see happen is that the its world view is proven wrong.

How does the ego seek to prevent you from realizing that there is an aspect of your world view and thought system (which form the filter through which you perceive life) that is wrong and needs to be revised? The effect of your mind state is that it causes you to identify with such outer things as your thought system. The ego seeks to make you feel that if your thought system is proven wrong, *you* are proven wrong— meaning there is something fundamentally wrong with you.

Consider how this affects people based on whether their mind state is dominated by black-and-white thinking or gray thinking. People dominated by black-and-white thinking will respond with fear and immediately think that if an aspect of their thought system is proven wrong, then they will suffer the worst fate defined by that thought system. For example, many fundamentalist Christians literally fear that if they were to accept that the earth is older than the 6,000 years defined by a literal interpretation of the Bible, then they will go to hell. That is a pretty powerful incentive for keeping your mind firmly closed to any idea that has not been approved as safe by the "infallible" or at least unquestionable authorities of your thought system. Many intellectual people will mock this fear-based approach to life, but they fail to see that their minds are equally closed—only they are trapped by pride instead of fear. What would happen to intellectual people if they were forced to consider that the materialistic world view is based on an illusion because there really is something beyond the material universe? Many would feel as if their entire world view or even their sense of identity would collapse. They might even fear – pride can be seen as a sophisticated way to ignore fear – that they would be ostracized by their fellow intellectuals or even lose their professional reputations, their jobs or their research grants. It can be difficult to get along in the scientific community if you are not a true-blood materialist. Going into an assembly of scientists and claiming that a material phenomenon has a non-material cause would expose you to much the same reaction as going into a fundamentalist church and claiming that the Bible is not the infallible word of God.

The ego will seek to keep your mind closed to new ideas by making you feel that if your old world view was proven wrong, then your worst fears would come to pass. You would either burn forever in hell or be banned from the materialist paradise on earth. If the ego can prevent you from acknowledging that you are wrong, you will never discover that the ego is wrong, and thus the ego can feel safe.

You are more than your beliefs

Once again, why are we not still living like cave men? Based on what we have learned about mind states, we can now gain a deeper understanding. A given mind state gives us a sense of identity, but this sense of identity is based on how we perceive the world. Our forefathers, the cave dwellers, had created a certain mind state based on the situation they faced and the way they looked at life. Once such a mind state has been created, it tends to become a closed system, a closed mental box, because it is difficult for us to question the perception upon which it is based. Why didn't our forefathers simply stay stuck in the mind state of being cave dwellers?

If our forefathers had stayed in that mind state – firmly identifying themselves as cave men and nothing more than cave men – how would we ever have risen above that stage? The simple answer is that we would still be living in caves, seeing ourselves as nothing more than cave dwellers. Obviously, we are no longer living like cave dwellers, which means there must be a mechanism that has caused us to rise above the mind state of the cave dwellers. What is that mechanism?

I earlier called it curiosity, the drive to know and understand how life works. I have also called it love, the tendency to be open towards life. We can now go deeper and realize that what has driven our progress is our intuitive faculties. These faculties allow us to "see" or "know" something that is beyond what the senses can detect or the intellect fathom. Our intuition helps us realize that we are more than our mind states, more than our beliefs about life, even more than our perception of life.

We expanded our understanding of life beyond what the cave dwellers knew by asking questions. Why did some people dare to ask such questions? In order to set your mind free from a certain mental box, you have to question the beliefs from which the box is built. You have to question at least certain aspects of your thought system.

If you have been brought up to believe that your thought system is infallible and gives you either all the knowledge you are allowed to have or all the knowledge there is, questioning your thought system means that you face a potentially very frightening shift in consciousness. In order to question your thought system, you have to be willing to consider that your thought system is either wrong or incomplete.

This can be frightening because it threatens the ego's sense of security and the ego will attempt to make you believe that it also threatens *your* security. In order to make the shift in consciousness that allows you to question your thought system, you have to use your intuitive faculties to come to a basic realization: You are more than your beliefs!

We could also say that you have to move from a frame of mind that is dominated by fear or pride into one that is dominated by love and curiosity.

How do you make that shift? Progress depends on our *ability* to ask questions, but the decisive factor is our *willingness* to ask questions beyond our current mental box. The foundation for asking such questions is the willingness to consider that our current mental box is either incorrect or incomplete, in other words the willingness to be proven wrong. When we are willing to be proven wrong, we open ourselves up to progress. When we are not willing to be proven wrong, we condemn ourselves to an indefinite stay in our current mental prison.

Are *we* truly proven wrong when one of our beliefs is proven wrong? If we have a limited belief about the world, and if that belief is proven wrong, we immediately open ourselves up to a higher understanding of life. How can that be a detriment to us? Consider that 500 years ago, the people in Europe believed the earth was flat. The stark reality was that the population of Europe had reached a level that was no longer sustainable by an agricultural society. There were so many people in medieval Europe that they could not all survive with the resources that could be grown on the land. Europe had hit a demographic ceiling. Here are the potential solutions to this problem:

• A reform of the feudal system so there was a more equal sharing of the available resources.

• An influx of new ideas and creativity that could open up for a leap from an agricultural society to an industrial society.

• A massive emigration so the surplus population in Europe went somewhere else.

The problem was that all three of these solutions were blocked by the mind states of medieval people, heavily influenced by Catholic doctrines and the world view that the earth was flat. The Catholic thought system upheld the feudal system and also prevented innovation. The belief in a flat earth prevented people from discovering new land beyond the borders of Europe.

The inevitable result was that there were too many people to be sustained by the system. Since the people would not reform the system, the only possible solution was that some people had to die.

In stepped the good old population reducers: disease, famine and war. The plague, starvation and continuous warfare kept the population at a sustainable level until the spell was broken and the old world view was questioned. When that finally happened, we saw a relatively quick transition that led from feudal societies to democracies, from an agricultural society to and industrial one and to the discovery of new land that absorbed much of the surplus population.

Did anyone actually lose from the fact that the old thought system was questioned and proven wrong? Yes, the people who were on top of the pyramid in the feudal system did in fact lose. The established power elite of the kings, the feudal lords and the infallible Catholic clergy lost their positions and privileges. Yet did the population lose, did humanity lose? To my mind, this was not a loss but a major step towards the awakening from the collective insanity.

Considering your true needs

If I asked you what your most important needs are, what would you answer? You will probably find that your needs can be fit into the pyramid of human needs defined by a psychologist named Abraham Maslow. He defined the basic human needs as follows (listed from lowest to higher needs):

- Physiological needs, relating to the survival and immediate security of the physical body.

- Safety and security needs, relating to the long-term survival of the body and also emotional stability.

- Love and belonging needs relating to our relationship with other people and the need to fit into a group.

- Esteem needs relating to how we are perceived by the group and how we are perceived by ourselves.

All of the above needs are what Maslow called deficit needs. We only notice these needs when they are *not* met—and in that case they can command our entire attention. If you feel you could be killed any moment by war, you have little attention left over for how you are perceived by your Facebook friends. If you find yourself trapped under water, breathing suddenly becomes much more important than eating.

As a side note, you might notice that physiological needs and security needs are tied to the emotion of fear. People who are focused on these needs are often very susceptible to black-and-white thinking. Love and belonging needs and esteem needs are more related to pride, and thus people focused on these needs are often more susceptible to gray thinking.

The term "deficit needs" indicates that even if all of these needs are met, they will still leave us feeling a deficit within us. As can be seen by observing the "rich and famous," having physical security, material abundance and the attention of the world is not enough to make you happy or give you peace of mind. We don't need celebrities to prove this to us because most of us are living proofs of it. In the Western world most people have grown up having their basic needs met. We have not actually had a deficit, but we have still experienced a deficit, as can be witnessed by the incredible amount of divorces, depressions, substance abuse problems, mental disorders and suicides.

The way out is to realize that the deficit needs are not our true needs. In order to find true happiness and peace of mind, we have to recognize a higher level of needs, namely what Maslow called self-actualization needs. According to Maslow, we human beings cannot be satisfied by living like animals— surviving, reproducing and belonging to the heard. We need more, namely a sense of who we are and why we are here.

The ego will seek to keep you trapped in the deficit needs forever. The reason is that the deficit needs are perfect for getting you to identify with your physical body, your pier group or your possessions or accomplishments in this world. What the ego loves about the deficit needs is that as long as they are not met, they tend to command your attention so you do not have any left over for even acknowledging your self-actualization needs.

As long as your mind is trapped into thinking that the goal of life is to fulfill your deficit needs, you are not likely to discover that your are more than the body, more than your beliefs, more than your mind state—the mind state dominated by unfulfilled and unfulfillable desires. You will not discover that you are more than your perception, which is also colored by deficit needs, even the very belief that life can only be a deficit. As long as you are trapped in the needs of this world, you will not discover that you – the you that has a need for self-discovery and self-actualization – is more than the ego.

Does this mean that we all have to have our deficit needs fulfilled to a certain level before we can discover our self-actualization needs? Not necessarily. In the West we do see a clear tendency that as society has become more affluent, more and more people have realized the limitations of a materialistic lifestyle and have started pursuing self-actualization needs. In the East, poverty was never a hindrance and a substantial percentage of the population was always pursuing these needs. The real issue is not the outer conditions, but an inner condition. In order to discover your self-actualization needs, you have to start questioning the mind state that is dominated by the deficit needs and the – often obsessive-compulsive – drive to fill them beyond what is possible. According to Maslow, deficit needs cannot actually be fulfilled in an ultimate way. They will always leave us feeling there is a deficit.

The underlying lie presented to you by the ego is that if only you fulfill the deficit needs to a critical degree, you will automatically be happy and have peace of mind. You will begin to overcome the magnetic pull of the deficit needs only by questioning this illusion. Once again, this questioning can happen as a result of the School of Hard Knocks or the School of Inner Awareness. In order to move from the hard knocks to awareness, you have to take the following step.

Restoring your natural curiosity

When we look at history and the fact that we have risen above past limitations, we might find reason for optimism. It seems that in the long run, love and curiosity win out over fear and pride. Fear and pride tend to create closed systems – from individual minds to world religions or political systems – yet an invisible natural force will, according to the second law of thermodynamics, cause them to self-destruct. Out of the ashes is born – as the phoenix bird – a new awareness that takes individuals and humanity to a higher level. It seems like an open mind driven by curiosity is our natural state whereas the closed mind, saturated with fear or pride, is an unnatural state for a human being.

Why do you – or people you know – face certain limitations that seemingly cannot be overcome or certain problems that seemingly cannot be solved? Our problems are the result of a limited understanding, and when we transcend that limited understanding, we begin to see solutions to our problems. We find this new understanding only through our curiosity, which means that the only way to rise above our current problems and limitations is to restart our curiosity.

You have to be willing to let go of the sense of security that is offered by your ego in exchange for staying in the mental box defined by the ego. People who are firmly convinced about the infallibility of their belief system seem to have a great sense of security. It is a rather vulnerable sense of security because if their thought system was proven wrong, it would instantly evaporate. The wise person seeks a deeper security that is not dependent upon anything outside yourself. The problem is that you cannot find such a sense of security unless you are willing to ask questions that go beyond your thought system, and that means letting go of the security offered by the system.

This can be quite difficult for people. For example, a fundamentalist Christian firmly believes that he is guaranteed to be saved. The condition is that he declares Jesus to be his Lord and Savior and accepts that the Bible is the infallible word of God. As long as he stays within that mental box, his ego will tell him that he is secure. Questioning one of the cornerstones of this thought system – such as the infallibility of the Bible – can be a very traumatic process.

Magnificent confusion

There is only one way to escape our current mind state. We must let go of our sense of security and throw ourselves into a state of insecurity that I would like to call "magnificent confusion." This expression jolts the mind into rethinking its concept of what it means to be confused. Normally, we think of confusion as something to be avoided like the plague. Our acceptance by our pier group is often closely tied to us never being confused about the thought system held by the group. Our self-esteem can be closely linked to the sense that we know a lot and have things figured out.

This sense of non-confusion is really a house built on the sand of a limited understanding. It is almost inevitable that it will be challenged at some point during our lifetime. Many people hold on to their sense of security as long as possible, but I believe many of us have already let go of it and have been willing to experience at least brief periods of magnificent confusion. We can become teachers who can help others move from fear and pride into love and curiosity.

I have personally experienced a number of periods in my life in which I was in magnificent confusion. These periods always opened me up to discovering a new and higher understanding of life. For about 20 years, this led me to discover a number of pre-defined thought systems. Each time I discovered a new system, it expanded my understanding. After a time, the system itself now began to limit my understanding because any system discourages questions that go beyond the system. I eventually came to a point where I was willing to let magnificent confusion become a way of life by accepting that no system can possibly capture the essence of life. Life is just too big to be fit into any system on earth.

There is great joy in allowing oneself to be magnificently confused. This is not a fear-based state of mind in which you feel threatened. It is a love-based state of mind in which you know that new discoveries await you around every bend in the road. I earlier mentioned Thomas Kuhn who discovered that scientific progress has two stages. One is the evolutionary stage in which scientists fill in the details of their current paradigm or world view. This can only take science so far, and progress will only happen when some scientists are willing to make a revolutionary leap that can take them to the next level.

Our personal progress happens the same way. There are periods where we fill in the details, but then there comes a point where we need to make a quantum leap. This requires us to pass through a period of magnificent confusion in which we acknowledge that we are willing to have our old beliefs proven wrong and we are willing to be delighted by new ideas.

How do we know when we are making a revolutionary leap? When we hear our egos roar like lions or slither like serpents in order to get us – by hook or by crook – to stay in the old fold. The ego has no problem with your evolutionary expansion of knowledge. If you have accepted a materialistic paradigm, the ego has no problem with you becoming an expert in physics, chemistry and biology. Try to question whether there is something beyond the material universe, and your ego will throw everything it has at you. Likewise, your ego has no problem with you becoming the most knowledgeable Christian on earth, but try to question whether Christianity is the only road to heaven, and your ego will give you a run for your money.

Let us dare to look beyond the human mental box and go through some magnificent confusion in order to discover new ideas about our true identity. Is it possible that we are actually more than human beings?

17 | WHAT ARE YOU?

We have so far talked about three levels of the human mind. One is the conscious mind where we make conscious decisions. Conscious decisions can be overridden by patterns in another level of the mind, namely the emotions. Emotions come from an even deeper layer, namely that of thoughts. A large part of the emotional and mental levels of the mind is below the threshold of conscious awareness and there is an elaborate process for filtering input. Ideas can be withheld from the conscious mind, which then prevents us from making the best possible decisions.

We have hinted that there might be a level of the mind that is beyond thought. Our basic perception of life will determine what we think and feel about life, and this mental and emotional reaction will create a certain mind state. Where does this basic perception come from? What determines our basic outlook on life?

This can be explained by defining a fourth level of the mind, namely that of identity. To many people – even many psychologists – this identity level will be unknown, and this is explained by our previous discussion. Our basic perception creates a mind state, and as long as we are fully identified with this state, we cannot question the basic perception that created it. We think our perception is not perception but reality, and we fail to see that our perception is actually formed at the highest level of the mind, namely where we find our sense of identity. As long as we are trapped in a mind state, we think our identity comes from that mind state or even from the outer conditions that the mind state finds all-important.

Your worldly sense of identity

If I ask you: "Who are you," what would you answer? You would probably begin with your name, as that has been programmed into our minds from childhood. These two or three words that have no real meaning are part of our sense of identity. Your next answer might be: "I am a man/woman." The sex of the physical body is an integral part of our sense of identity. At the next level would probably come factors such as your race, ethnicity, religion or nationality. Then might come your profession or education, maybe your political affiliation.

There is nothing wrong with having a sense of identity as I just described. It is a practical part of life on this planet. However, the factors we have looked at above all have something in common. They are all designed to make it easy to identify you as a person set apart from all other human beings. The above identifiers are all distinct, meaning they are localized. While this is fine for practical reasons, it also has some potential dangers. Almost any aspect of these outer identifiers can be used by the ego to come up with a value judgment that says some people are better than others.

For most people the identifiers represent something final. This is who we are, and there is nothing we can do about it. If our identifiers seem to create an irreconcilable conflict between our group and another group, then the only resolution we can see is that the other group must submit or disappear. Because the identifiers seem absolute, the value judgment imposed upon them also seems absolute, which is why most people never question it.

Is it truly necessary that there should be an inherent conflict between men and women or that women should be seen as inferior, meaning they must submit to men? Is it necessary that some people with a particular last name should be considered better than others? Is it necessary that people of a particular religion think they are better than all non-members, setting up an inherent conflict with the members of other religions who feel the same way? Or look at some of the other conflicts that have come up because of such localized identifiers—even the fans of two soccer clubs can seem to be in irreconcilable conflict that can spill over into violence.

An identity that is beyond evil

All human evil – and the collective insanity in general – comes from certain mind states. These mind states are the byproducts of a localized sense of identity. If we are to ever go beyond evil, we have to go beyond the localized identifiers and find a way to identify ourselves that is non-local, meaning that it is based on what we have in common rather than what sets us apart.

I am not hereby saying that our localized identity is evil. I am saying that the ego and the power elite can use our localized identity to manipulate us into conflict with other people. Identifying ourselves as belonging to a group of people who – as a result of their identity – are locked in conflict with another group of people is indeed the cause of much evil. There is only one way to rise above this, and it is to realize and experience that we are more than our localized identity. There is more to you, there is a higher part of your identity, than your localized self.

Let me give an example of how our sense of identity gives rise to mind states. Let us say you have been brought up to identify yourself as a Catholic. You believe that being a Catholic virtually guarantees your entry into the kingdom of heaven whereas all non-Catholics will go to hell. This sense of being saved is based on the religion of the Catholic Church having a certain authority, almost infallibility. At the very deepest level of your mind, a filter is created. Any information that affirms the validity of the Catholic religion is labeled as good, useful or even true. Any information that seems to challenge or question the Catholic Church is labeled as bad, dangerous, useless or false. Any challenging information is likely filtered out by the intellect before it even reaches your conscious mind. This explains why Catholics can look at history without actually "seeing" the burning of books, the crusades, the massacre of the Cathars, the Inquisition the witch hunts, the suppression of scientists and other undeniable historical facts.

I have talked to Catholics who literally do not see these events or do not see them as significant. In these people's minds, nothing that the Catholic Church has ever done or could ever do will shake their basic faith in the Church and their own salvation. I once watched a television special on the sex-abuse scandal in the Diocese of Boston. It was centered on a man who had been sexually abused by a Catholic priest as a teenager and who had been emotionally scarred for life. The man's parents were still tried and true Catholics. Even when their local church building was sold by the Diocese in order to raise money for the retributions they were ordered to pay, these people's loyalty to the Church was not shaken. They could not conceive of themselves as not being Catholic.

Please note that I am not trying to bash Catholics or the Catholic Church. I am simply pointing out how a strong identifier creates a filter that affects people's perception. People literally see only certain things and completely overlook certain others. Once a strong filter has been created at the identity level, people's perception at the lower levels of thoughts and feelings literally sees only what the filter wants them to see. If you identify yourself as a Catholic, you only see the good things that the Catholic Church has done and you overlook the not so good.

Let us now flip this over to the other side. Take people who are negative towards the Catholic Church in particular or all religion in general. Such people also have a filter at the identity level, and it has the reverse effect of the Catholic filter. They perceive only the bad things that the Catholic Church (or all religion) has done while completely overlooking the many good things that the Church (or all religion) has done. A clear proof of this is that there are people who believe that all human conflict is caused by religion. I personally find it very hard to "see" the Roman emperors, the Viking raiders, Ivan the Terrible, Karl Marx, Lenin, Stalin, Hitler and Pol Pot as people who were motivated by religion.

As another example, we can go back to my experience with Jews and Palestinians. They both have a localized sense of identity and it affects the way they perceive their situation. Palestinians tend to overlook anything good done by individual Jews or by the state of Israel, while seeing everything that is or even seems bad. Jews, of course tend to have the opposite filter, many of them thinking that the state of Israel could not possibly do anything wrong. We can find numerous examples of similar conflicts where the two sides have a completely different perception of the situation. I once watched a television program about how officers in the German army had perceived the second world war, and it was very different from the way I had been brought up to see it.

How our sense of identity creates conflict

The conflicts we see among both individuals and groups of people are on the surface level caused by certain mind states. Certain groups of people have a mind state of being victims, which means they are looking for an oppressor to affirm this mind state. They literally *want* to be persecuted because that affirms their basic outlook on life. Other groups have a mind state in which they want to feel superior and want to dominate so they naturally attract to themselves a group who wants to be dominated. We then have the classical co-dependent relationship between perpetrator and victim—none of these mind states being able to exist without the other.

Palestinians represent one mind state and Jews another. Catholics represent one mind state and anti-religious people another. Manchester United fans represent one mind state and Liverpool fans another. The husband of a typical marriage represents one mind state and the wife another—and so on ad naseum.

When you look at the mind states alone, there is absolutely no way to reconcile the conflicts between groups of people or individuals. How can you create a reconciliation when the two sides literally "see" something different when they look at the same situation?

We can either give up, or we can apply the old technique of seeking to expand our understanding. In this case, we can realize that a mind state is the byproduct of the conditions found at a higher level of the mind, namely where our sense of identity is defined. We can then look at the factors that make up our sense of identity, identify the ones that are localized, and now we see the real cause of evil. We can then look beyond these localized identifiers and look for a way to identify ourselves that is non-local. Obviously, this is the last thing the ego wants us to do, as its very reason for being is to actually define and preserve our localized sense of identity.

Who are you, really?

There is a very intriguing story about the life of the Buddha, a story that can teach us something about ourselves. The Buddha was born into a royal family, and for the first many years of his life, his father took great pains to prevent the young prince from seeing anything negative or ugly. The inside of the palace was very beautiful and the prince saw only young and healthy people. The father was seeking to control the prince's perception of life so he would think life was only beautiful and comfortable.

In early adulthood, the prince took a walk outside the palace and came across a decrepit old man. Upon seeing the signs of decay and death, the prince's mental box was shattered and he immediately began to question his perception of life. As a result, he left the palace behind and withdrew to the forest where he spent six years living the austere life of an ascetic monk, often sitting so long in meditation that the birds built nests in his beard.

After six years of this, the young man suddenly had a realization. In a flash he "saw" that the ascetic form of life would not bring him the inner peace he was seeking. Instead, he saw that the only road to inner peace was something he called the "Middle Way." As a result of this realization, the young man awakened to Buddhahood and spent some time in a higher state of consciousness, called Nirvana. After a time, he decided to go out into the world and teach others what he had realized. After coming back to the world, he first encountered a group of peasants. They sensed there was something special about the Buddha, so instead of asking the normal question: "*Who* are you," they asked: "*What* are you?" To which the Buddha answered: "I am awake!"

I believe that the way this story it is told in mainstream Buddhism is destructive to the Buddha's original purpose and intention. The story portrays the Buddha exactly the same way as the story of Jesus' birth portrays him, namely as a being who is so different from the rest of us that we could not possibly do what Jesus or the Buddha did. Let me give a different slant on the story of the Buddha.

The Buddha's father can be seen as a symbol for the ego. While we are in the unawakened state, the ego is the king of our world. The palace in which the young prince grew up is a symbol for the mental box created by the ego. The ego does not want us to leave the mental box, and in order to ensure this, the ego seeks to control our perception of life. The ego does not want us to discover anything that might cause us to question the value of the mental box or the perception upon which it is built.

The story of the Buddha is – potentially – the story of all of us. Most of the people who are open to this book will have gone through the same steps as the young Buddha. We grew up in the modern world that is similar to a palace in which everything is beautiful and affluent and in which we are shielded from seeing decay, poverty and death. At some point in our lives, we realized that life inside this palace simply wasn't enough for us. There had to be more to life, and we decided to leave the palace—at least mentally. We started studying teachings and ideas that were very different from the ones used to build the palace. Some of us even started questioning the basic perception of life upon which the palace was built.

So far, we have followed the same inner process as the one experienced by the Buddha—and also by Jesus if you read between the lines. The question is whether we have yet fully awakened from the mental box in which our identity is trapped. If you have not fully awakened, I suggest you might make decisive progress by considering what I have said in previous chapters about perception and mental states. You will make even more progress by coming to the same realization as the Buddha, namely that reality is beyond the dualistic view of the world.

It is somewhat unfortunate that the Buddha's original concept has generally been translated as the "Middle Way." To the intellectual, linear mind, it sounds like the Middle Way is found in the midpoint between two extremes. Many people look at the Buddha, and they see that he first grew up in one extreme, namely an entirely materialistic lifestyle. He then saw the fallacy of this and went into the exact opposite, namely an ascetic lifestyle that denies all material comforts, even denies the body. Then he awakened and now advocated a way that seems to be in the midway point between the two extremes, namely a more balanced approach to life. I am not disagreeing that the Buddha's way is a balanced approach to life. Yet this balance is not attained by finding a midpoint between two extremes. It is attained in an entirely different way.

The unreality of locality

When the Buddha had his "Aha experience" in the forest, he saw that the key to peace is not found in this extreme, nor in the opposite extreme, nor at any point in between the two extremes. He saw the unreality of the entire consciousness of separation that divides reality into separate compartments. He saw the unreality of the dualistic mindset that creates a scale where everything has to be fit on a line between the two opposite polarities. He saw that peace cannot be found at any point on this relative scale, not even in the mid-point between the two extremes. Peace can be found only by transcending the entire scale and the dualistic consciousness that makes it seem real and makes it seem like the only way to approach life. When you do transcend this mindset, you see that the appearance of divisions and opposites is just that—an appearance. When you see beyond this illusion – the "veil of Maya," as the Buddha called it – you see the one underlying reality. The Buddha expressed it this way: "Everything is the Buddha Nature."

We can find a very similar concept in most of the world's spiritual teachings. For example, the *Gospel of John* opens with the following: "In the beginning was the Word, and the Word was with God, and the Word was God. And without Him was not any thing made which was made." The correct translation would be to use "Logos" instead of "Word," Logos signifying an underlying, unifying principle. All true spiritual teachers have attempted to help us see that locality is an illusion and that reality truly is non-local.

What did the Buddha mean when he said: "I am awake?" He meant that he had awakened from the illusion of duality and separation. Compare this to the first verse of the main Buddhist scripture. The first concept that the Buddha introduces is perception, which implies that he considered it extremely important. What the Buddha was truly saying is that when you approach life with polluted perception, you will perceive life as suffering. Only when you approach life with unpolluted perception, will you experience peace and happiness.

Polluted perception is perception based on the illusion of locality and separation, which makes it seem like life has to be put on a scale with two relative opposites. When you perceive life this way, you create a mind state that pulls you towards one extreme or the other. For example, most people in the world are pulled into focusing on the material aspects of life. Some people eventually come to see the limitations of a materialistic lifestyle, and they are then pulled into the opposite extreme, namely a so-called spiritual or ascetic lifestyle that renounces all materiality. A few people eventually come to see the limitations of this approach and now either give up or seek some compromise between the two.

What the Buddha, Jesus and all other true spiritual teachers offer us is an alternative, namely a grand awakening so we free our minds from the entire relative scale. We transcend the opposites – what the Buddha called "the pairs" – and instead grasp the underlying unity of all life. When we perceive life through this unpolluted – non-dual, non-relative – perception, we will not create mind states but will keep our minds free from the many traps created by the ego—what Jesus called "the prince of this world." When our minds are free from duality and relativity, we can say like Jesus did: "The prince of this world comes and has nothing in me." When our minds contain no elements of the dualistic perception, there is nothing whereby the magnetic force of the ego or the power elite can pull us back into the collective insanity. *That* is the foundation for true inner peace and happiness.

Non-local awareness

So *who* or *what* are we? The first thing we notice is that we have
the ability to ask that question. Our ability to ask questions
has brought us from the cave man stage to modern humans,
and that shows us we are neither cave men nor modern people. If we had been the kind of creatures that human beings
outpictured during the age of the cave man, we would never
have risen above that stage. There are still some animals that
were alive when the cave dwellers roamed the earth, and they
have not evolved beyond that point. We have evolved very far
beyond the cave man stage, and that shows us there is a part of
our identity that is not set in stone.

We human beings do not have a fixed sense of identity.
There must be a flexible core of our identity that can see itself
as many different types of beings. Just look at the world today
and see how many different types of people you find. Some of
them are completely identified with a very limited stage, such
as people who identify themselves with the physical body or a
limited state of existence. Consider the range in identity from
a psychopath, totally focused on himself, to a highly altruistic
person who works selflessly to serve others.

The existence of mind states explains many of these differences, but mind states come from the identity level of the
mind. Even at the identity level, there must be a part of our
identity that is not fixed. A sense of identity takes a particular
form, such as "man," "woman," "American," "Muslim" etcetera. There must be part of our identity that is beyond such
forms. There must be part of our identity that is non-local in
nature.

This idea will challenge the traditional thought systems that
seek to tell us who we are. Christianity wants us to believe that
we are fundamentally flawed, that we are "created" as sinners.

Materialism want us to think we are merely evolved apes and that our identity is predetermined by our genes and our upbringing. Neither thought system can explain how humanity has risen from the primitive stage to our present level or how individuals can grow up in very difficult circumstances and still rise above them. According to both, there should be limits to our ability to rise, but if we honestly observe life, we see that this is challenged by facts. It is true that the majority of human beings do seem to grow up with a certain fixed sense of identity and do not rise above it for the rest of their lives. Yet there are numerous examples of people who did actually go very far beyond what they should have been capable of according to their upbringing.

Once again, we can pull the power elite out of the closet and realize that if a small elite is to be successful in controlling the general population, the very foundation is to get the population to accept that their sense of identity is determined by factors over which they have no control. If people accept a limited sense of identity – such as belonging to a lower class of peasants – they will never be able to challenge their noble overlords. This was a major factor behind the longevity of the feudal societies.

The ego is also a major factor. If we do have a fixed sense of identity, then there really isn't much you can do to change your life. You simply have to accept your lot in life and live as comfortably as you can within the mental box defined by the power elite and your ego. Don't rock the boat, just live like everyone else. Precisely because this will make the ego feel secure, this can be a comfortable lifestyle, far more comfortable than accepting your potential to rise above your "assigned" station in life. Yet is it enough for you to live this way? If it had been, you would not have been reading this book.

18 | THE WAY TO OVERCOME EVIL

What is the foundation for our ability to ask the question: "What are we?" It is the very fact that we are conscious, that we have self-awareness. We have the ability to step back and consider who or what we are instead of being fully absorbed in acting out who we are. As far as we know, no animal species has this self-awareness. Lions do not see themselves as lions and they do not think, feel or sing like humans (despite what the Disney Corporation seeks to make us believe).

The French philosopher René Descartes made the famous statement: "I think, therefore I am." What he meant was that the very fact that we can think proves that we exist. We could twist his statement and say: "I am, therefore I can think," meaning that I exist – I have being – and that is what gives me the foundation for thinking. Thoughts exist at a surface level of the mind, and when we go to deeper levels, we encounter a state of pure being, pure existence. Thinking is focused on an object – we are thinking about something – but beyond that is pure awareness, meaning awareness without an object.

Some readers will immediately understand what I am saying because they have experienced pure or non-local awareness. Others have not experienced it, and thus the concept will sound abstract. All I am asking you to do here is to make a very slight shift in your awareness.

Up until now, you have been reading this book, and you have probably been absorbed in thinking about its contents— or perhaps something else. I am now asking you to mentally step back and realize that you are sitting here, reading this book. I am asking you to envision that "you" are standing outside your body and mentally looking at your body sitting wherever you are and holding this book. Now consider a simple question. You have two elements of this situation. You have the object, which is the body holding the book, and then you have the you who is observing the body. Who is the "you" that is doing the observing?

Let us take another example. This planet has an amazing variety of environments. You have probably grown up in a particular environment, and this is what you have experienced as the center of your world. What is the "you" that is experiencing your environment? It must be a form of consciousness, yet is it tied to your environment? If you traveled to a very different environment, would you suddenly become unconscious? Obviously not, which proves that there is a part of your awareness that can experience any type of environment.

Wherever you go on this planet, you will still be conscious, which proves that the "you" that is conscious is non-localized because it is able to experience any type of localized environment. Compare this to what I said earlier that the words you are reading can exist only because of the white page behind them. We are normally completely focused on the contents of our consciousness—in fact, in the Western world the contents is all that is recognized. Behind the contents is something that allows the contents to exist. Behind the contents of your consciousness is a state of mind without objects—pure awareness. In the East, and also in the Western tradition, mystics have been studying consciousness and experiencing pure awareness for thousands of years.

Because your native environment is very familiar to you and probably feels comfortable and secure, it is likely that you have developed a mind state in which you see yourself as a being living in that environment. This is your localized self. If you moved to another environment, your mind state or sense of identity would move with you. For example, when I moved from my native Denmark to the United States, I at first saw myself as a Dane living in America. It took several years before I started seeing myself as an American, and in a sense I have never fully accepted myself as an American. Instead, I developed a sense of identity as a universal being who is not identified based on the country in which I live at present.

Despite the fact that we grow up with a localized sense of identity, we can adapt to different conditions. We can – at least theoretically – adapt to any environment found on this planet. Once again, we see that there is a core of our identity that is non-local in nature. This is the only explanation for the fact that we can experience and adapt to so many different localized circumstances.

You have heard about the concept of "survival of the fittest," and you probably think the fittest are those who have certain fixed qualities that make them superior. The dinosaurs became extinct when the climate cooled because they were not able to adapt to the changing environment. The warm-blooded and smaller mammals were better suited to adapting, and that is why they survived and took over the earth. The most *fit* are the most *adaptable,* and there is no other life form that is as adaptable as human beings.

We can live in more environments than any animal species, and the reason is that we are able to consciously change our behavior depending on the environment. We can even change our behavior in ways that change the environment. It is our adaptability that makes us the most fit species on earth, and our adaptability comes from the fact that there is a core of our beings that is non-local and therefore can adapt itself to and express itself through a wide variety of environments and circumstances. Of course, these considerations would not be complete without looking at another factor in our adaptability, namely our *willingness* to adapt—or the lack of it.

The enigma of free will

Some philosophers have made a career out of debating whether we really have free will. I am not going to go into a detailed argument about free will. Experience has shown me that there are some people who will vehemently deny that we have free will and who will come up with all kinds of intellectual arguments that they think are more valid than the obvious counter-arguments. When I ask them if the very fact that they can deny free will doesn't prove that they have free will (because if you didn't have free will, why would it even be a question for debate?), they will simply ignore it and come up with a sophisticated intellectual argument.

When you know the characteristics of the ego, it is easy to see why some people will not acknowledge the reality of free will. These people have bought into the sense of identity created by their egos. They are comfortable in believing that their identities were determined by external factors and that they cannot drastically change their lives. If they were to accept free will, they would have to consider that they are who they are because of choices they have made and not because of external factors. They would also have to consider that they can change themselves and their lives.

Some people are not ready to take responsibility for their lives, and they will deny free will until that changes. Such people obviously are not the ones who can help awaken the world from the collective insanity, and thus I am not seeking to convince them. Instead, I will focus on working with the people who are willing to take responsibility and realize the universal timeless truth that the way to change the world is to begin by changing ourselves.

We can change ourselves precisely because we have free will and self-awareness—and because these are non-localized qualities. Self-awareness allows us to mentally step outside our normal mind state and sense of identity. We can look at our localized self and ask: "It this the kind of being I want to be?" If the answer is that we want to be more, then our self-awareness gives us the ability to imagine that more. Our free will gives us the ability to consciously and deliberately change our sense of self. This is the real mechanism that has brought us beyond the cave-man stage: Our ability to consciously change our localized self, which then automatically changes the way we look at life, the way we think about life, the way we feel about life and the way we act in life.

Both official Christianity and materialistic science say that our localized self is beyond our capacity to change. It is either created by God or a product of "nature and nurture." In my opinion one of the most significant developments of the past century is the emergence of a movement we might call the self-help movement. It is based on a recognition of the fact that we do indeed have the option to consciously and willfully change

ourselves. The basis for this free will is that there is a core of
our beings that is non-local in nature, meaning that it is not a
product of external conditions. The basis for any form of self-
help is that instead of simply adapting to existing conditions,
we can take command over our conditions. We do not need
to be slaves of the past but can change our future for the better. Some think self-help is just psycho-babble, but then please
explain to me how we have risen from the primitive stage to
where we are today.

To me, our progress unequivocally proves that we do have
the ability to consciously and willfully change our circumstances. This ability comes from the fact that we have the ability to change our localized self. We can do this because we also
have a non-localized self that can imagine itself as more than
the localized self and which has the will to change the localized
self according to its vision.

First, change your identity

There is a particular approach to changing your circumstances
that is far more efficient than any other. Some people seek
to change their actions by only working with the level of the
conscious mind. Actions spring from emotions so if you do
not seek to change the emotions, your attempts to change your
actions will be an uphill battle and will run into some limitations. You will go further by working with your emotions also,
but then again, feelings come from thoughts. In order to be
more efficient, you also need to change your thinking.

Thoughts and feelings form a mind state that can have a
profound impact on how we see – perceive – everything in life.
To truly be efficient in changing your life, you need to examine
your mind state and the perception that created it. This leads

us to the deepest level of the outer mind, namely the level of identity.

There is a hierarchical structure to the mind, and your conscious actions are at the bottom of the food chain. If you really want to change your life, the most efficient way is to go directly to the top and change your sense of identity, meaning how you see yourself and how you see life. When you make a change at that level, it will filter down to the lower levels. You may still have to examine thought and feeling patterns as well as physical habits, but it will be far easier to make changes at the lower levels once you have changed the top level. When you seek to make a change at a lower level, you still have the impulse coming from the higher levels of the mind, which means you are fighting against yourself. You are a house divided against itself.

As an example, take the organization Alcoholics Anonymous. I am in no way trying to question the fact that it has helped countless people. Every person I have met who has gone through AA has told me the same thing: People are told to see themselves as alcoholics for life. They are recovering alcoholics, and they have learned to overcome the desire to drink, but they still have that desire. To me, this indicates that AA does not go to the very top layer of the mind. It does not seek to raise people's sense of identity; it affirms a limited sense of identity, namely as a life-long alcoholic.

Even though many people do avoid drinking, it comes at a high cost, namely that they must constantly fight the urge to drink. The ultimate freedom from alcoholism is that you are completely free from any urge to drink. This can be accomplished by changing your sense of identity so that you come to see yourself as a person who is fully capable of dealing with whatever circumstances life serves up. You know that you have no need to run away from anything, which means you no longer have a need for escape. When this change in your sense of identity is complete, you no longer see yourself as an alcoholic, not even as a recovered alcoholic. You see yourself as a being for whom drinking is unnecessary, perhaps even unthinkable.

Our options for exercising free will

Let me summarize our findings:

- The underlying cause of conflict and personal unhappiness is that our egos have managed to create a sense of identity that presents us as localized, separate beings who are threatened by other people and life circumstances.

- We are more than the ego and more than the ego's sense of identity.

- That "more" is a level of our beings that is non-localized in nature and is independent of any form or condition in the material world.

- This non-local self is where our free will is located, or at least where it can potentially be located.

We have two options for exercising our free will. One is to allow ourselves to be fully absorbed in and identified with the localized self. This means our perception of life is colored by the subconscious filters. This polluted perception gives rise to certain mind states that overpower our free will. We are not making truly free choices because we are basing our choices on the way we perceive life through the localized filter. If we base our choices on incorrect or incomplete information, how can we make truly free choices?

When we make such unfree choices, all of our choices will have undesirable consequences. Not only does this turn our lives into a constant struggle, but it can even give us the sense that we do not want to make choices. This is what causes some people to deny free will. What is the point in making choices if you are damned when you do and damned when you don't?

We have an alternative to making these unfree choices. We have the potential to reconnect to the non-local part of our beings and come to see life without the localized filter. We can then perceive things in a different way, which makes is possible for us to use our free will in a way that is, well: free.

The fear of death

At this point, your ego might be screaming that what I am saying is dangerous. You might even feel an emotion that is the deepest feeling of the localized self, namely the fear of death. This is the most basic fear of human beings and that is why it is the primary tool used by the power elite and our egos in order to control us. Where does the fear of death come from? It comes from the localized self; it was born with the localized self.

We have now come to the realization I have been leading up to throughout this book. I have said that the mind has a hierarchical structure with several layers. At the bottom is the mind that is focused on the physical body and our actions. Above that is the level of emotions, above that thoughts and finally we have the level of identity. The level of identity has two layers.

Throughout history, some people have decided to explore the layers of their minds. They have often been called mystics and they can be found within all religious traditions and also independently of any outer religion. What the mystics of the world have all realized is that when you go into the identity level of the mind, you first encounter the localized self. This localized self is a formidable challenge for the mystic because our identification with it is so strong.

When you persist in projecting yourself beyond the localized self, questioning all aspects of it, you will come to a direct experience of what is often called a mystical state of mind. It has been called by many specific names, but the importance is that this is a non-localized state of mind. You are not observing from without – as you do through the separate self – you are directly experiencing that you are a non-local being. When you have had this experience even once – and when you have acknowledged having the experience – your fear of death is gone forever.

What the mystics of the world have all reported is that when you go beyond the localized self, you experience yourself as a non-local being. Your are not theorizing about what this being is and what characteristics it has. You are experiencing it, and this experience is far more real than anything you experienced through the mind state, the perception filter, of the localized self. It is literally as if you had been wearing colored contact lenses all of your life, and now you have taken them off, experiencing life without a filter.

What you experience as the non-local self is that you are beyond death. You know you cannot die and thus your fear of death is gone. How is this possible? Because you have now experienced that you are not the localized self, you are more than the localized self—and only a localized self can die. The localized self is by its very nature confined to time and space. It exists in a particular space and at a particular time. This means that the localized self can – indeed, *must* – die. Everything that is localized has a beginning and must have an end. Death is the price we pay for taking on a localized self.

If you are open to this book, you are probably open to some form of spiritual world view. You probably believe that you are more than your physical body because you have a soul that has entered the body and resides there only for a time. You might believe that this soul will not die when the physical body dies, as most spiritual and religious people believe.

I am now asking you to go one step further. What most people call the soul is what I call the localized self. The physical body is a vehicle that the soul uses for expressing itself in the material world. The soul – made up of the four levels of the mind – is a vehicle through which the non-local self expresses itself in the material world. The highest level of the soul is the sense of identity, but even this is localized and thus mortal. Yet this self – however persistent the illusion might be – is not who you really are.

The awakening of the non-local self

There are spiritual teachings that say the existence of an individual self is an illusion because there is only one self, one mind. They say this individual self must die in order for us to be enlightened. My experience is that this is too extreme of an interpretation. The reality is that there is a localized self and a non-localized self. The localized self must die, but the non-local self must awaken to its true identity as an individualized expression of the one mind.

If life is to have any meaning, then the material world is a vehicle for our expansion of consciousness. William

Shakespeare said: "All the world's a stage," meaning that the material world is like a theater. You are like an actor and your purpose is to select a role in the theater and experience life through it until you have had enough. At that point, you can select another role, and you can continue to do this until you have had enough of the theater itself. The individual roles you play and the actions you take are not significant in themselves. What is significant is the effect that playing a role has on your non-local sense of self. For each localized role you play, your non-local self grows in awareness of itself—what it *is* and what it is *not*.

You play a certain role in the theater of life by taking on not just a physical body but also a localized self. Although physical bodies have individual characteristics, they also have similarities. A certain type of male body can take many different types of actions, depending on which soul is inhabiting a specific body. For example, a strong muscular body can be a fierce warrior but also a gentle giant. In order to have a particular kind of experience through a physical body, you need a localized self that serves as an interface between your non-local self and the body.

In order to truly experience the role, your non-local self enters into the localized self as the localized self enters the body. Once inside, you perceive life through the filter of the localized self and the senses of the body. All of us have gone through this process, and in the beginning stages of the journey, we become so identified with the body and the localized self that we forget that we actually are a non-local self. As we progress on our journey, we gradually begin to awaken from this illusion. We begin to feel we have had enough of the roles defined in the theater and we begin to reconnect to some sense of non-locality.

The highest cause of evil

Once again, what is the cause of evil? The localized self is not evil in and of itself. I would not even say that the localized self is the cause of evil. Evil is identification with the localized self to the point where you believe killing or controlling another human being is justified by some goal defined by the localized self.

The entire purpose for life on this planet is that a non-local self has an experience through a localized self and a physical body. Killing that physical body deprives the non-local self of its opportunity to grow in self-awareness, and since this defies the very purpose of life, it is a form of evil. Beyond this is an attempt to kill the localized self, the soul vehicle, and this is the ultimate form of evil.

What can make a person believe that *killing* the soul vehicle of another person is necessary or justified? What can make a person believe that *saving* the soul vehicle of another person is necessary or justified? It is ultimate identification with your own localized self. You may then believe that the survival of your localized self is threatened by another localized self, and in order to survive, you have to kill the other. You may also believe that the survival of another localized self is threatened and thus it is necessary for you to control the other soul for its own salvation. Whatever the motivation or the belief, we now see a new definition of evil.

The purpose of the material world is to function as a stage on which non-local selves can outplay various roles in order to grow in self-awareness. What guides the growth of a particular non-local self is its free will. The ultimate form of evil is to control or neutralize the free will of another self-aware being. This form of evil becomes possible only when you identify yourself fully with and as your localized self. Only the localized self can feel threatened by other selves having free will and exercising it as they see fit.

When I have a direct experience that I am a non-local self, I overcome all fear of death. I experience that I am more than my localized self. I know that if my physical body dies, *I* will not die. I know that even if my localized self dies, *I* will not die. This means I cannot feel ultimately threatened by anything that happens in the material world. If I do not feel threatened, I cannot fall prey to the illusion that in order to protect my life or my sense of security, it is justifiable to kill or control you. I can, in the ultimate sense, live and let live.

Overcoming evil

When I experience that *I* am a non-local self, I also know that at the core of *your* identity is a non-local self. I experience myself as an expression of the One Non-Local Self, and I know you too are an expression of that same self. We are two waves on the same ocean. How can I kill or control a being who is an expression of the same One Self from which I sprang? It simply isn't possible, but it is impossible only because now I do not see you through polluted perception, the perception of the localized self.

I am not hereby saying that we will lose the localized self. As long as we are in physical embodiment, we will need a localized self as a vehicle for expression. You do not have to shave your head, forsake your family and live in the forest in order to overcome evil. Evil is identification with the localized self. When you experience yourself as a non-local self, you can no longer identify yourself with or as the localized self. Your localized self now becomes something that is similar to your car.

You may like your car, but you do not believe that by getting into your car, you become the car. You know you can always get out of your car and that you can live without it (perhaps not without *any* car, but without a *specific* car). Your car is just a vehicle that you use in getting from place to place—and so is your localized self.

When you awaken from identification with your localized self, you will have overcome evil in yourself. When enough people awaken and begin to talk about and demonstrate their non-local sense of self, we will have an impact on society as a whole. This does not mean that we will instantly eradicate evil. When you awaken from locality, you see that it is not your role to help destroy or eradicate evil.

You see that it is actually part of evil to define something as good and evil and then seek to force other people to accept your definition—killing those who refuse. You even see that what the localized self defines as good is not good in a non-local sense. It is only what is good for the localized self; it is what is good *relative* to the localized self. What the localized self sees as good and evil is a product of its perception, and since you no longer identify with the perception of your localized self, you are not blinded by it.

You now realize that eradicating evil does not in any way make it necessary to force, control or kill other people. The way to overcome evil is *not* to define something as evil and then seek to destroy it. The way to overcome evil is to transcend the entire mind state in which reality must be divided into two opposite polarities.

Our role in the world is *not* to fight other people or belief systems. Our role is to first free ourselves from the illusion of the localized self and then help others do the same. We do this not by seeking to force or control others but by demonstrating that there is a better way to live. Some will not be ready because they still want to experience life through the localized self. We need to respect this but we also need to respect our right to demonstrate a higher form of life regardless of the fact that some people are disturbed by it. We have a right to be non-local and a right to allow others to be local.

19 | DO WE HAVE A PSYCHOLOGY OF EVIL?

Have we made progress towards a psychology of evil? I believe we have because we have discovered that the cause of evil is entirely psychological.

Traditionally, the discussion around evil has tended to focus at the level of action. It is easy to identify certain actions as evil, but this gives us limited options for overcoming evil. It is difficult enough to change your own actions, but an entirely different matter to change the actions of other people.

Seeking to change others easily leads to an attempt to force them, and this creates resistance. The result might be a fight to the death, but did we not start out our quest to overcome evil because we thought killing others was evil? What sense does it make that in order to overcome evil, we are now engaged in doing what we have defined as evil?

A new model of the psyche

Even though actions are physical, their cause is psychological. We have seen that the mind, or psyche, can be divided into four layers:

- The lowest level is the physical mind or the level of action. We can clearly identify certain actions as evil, but actions do not appear in a vacuum. They are caused by patterns in the higher levels of the mind. For most people, their conscious minds are largely tied to or identified with the level of the physical body and actions. Many people have little awareness of what leads them to commit certain actions, meaning they have little power to consciously change their actions.

- The next level up is that of emotions. Most people have certain patterns in the emotional level of the mind, patterns that prevent us from making entirely free choices as to how we respond to certain situations. Many people have such a spiral of anger in their emotions that their default reaction to most situations is anger. Emotions fall into two categories, namely those based on love and those based on fear. Evil actions are triggered by fear-based emotions. Emotions are not the ultimate cause of evil because emotions are effects of what is happening at the next level up.

- The level of the mind that is above emotions is the mental level or the realm of thoughts. For most people, especially in the Western world, thoughts are dominated by the intellect. The intellect is an analytical faculty, meaning it processes new information by comparing it to an existing database that for most people resides below the level of conscious awareness. It is possible that the intellect can filter out certain thoughts and impressions before they reach the conscious mind. This explains why people can fail to see that their actions contradict some of their beliefs. For example, it explains why a person can oversee the killing of Jewish children in Auschwitz while making no connection between them and his own children. Thoughts come from an even higher level of the mind.

• Above thought is the level of identity, our deepest sense of who we are. Our sense of identity defines the parameters for our subconscious databases. Given that identity is above thoughts, emotions and actions, it will define what happens at the lower levels. Our identity has two distinct spheres. One is the separate or localized self that identifies itself as separated from its source, from its environment and from other separate selves. The other is the non-local self which empowers us to experience oneness with our source, our environment and with other people.

Evil truly is a product of the localized self. Only this self can believe that I can harm or control you without this having negative consequences for myself. Only when I see you and I as completely separate beings, can this illusion seem believable. Separation truly is an illusion. Modern science has disproved locality and has indicated the existence of a collective consciousness to which all people are tied. This has been taught by mystical teachers for thousands of years.

With this model of the psyche, we have opened up new hope for the possibility of overcoming human evil. It is possible for an individual to raise his or her sense of identity above that of the localized self. By reconnecting to our non-local identity, we begin to experience a deeper sense of oneness with each other, and this makes it impossible for one person to harm another.

Because we are all tied through the collective consciousness, one person rising above the illusion of locality and dualism will have an uplifting effect on the whole. Once a critical mass is reached, a shift can occur, as seen with the abolishment of slavery and the emergence of democracy. It it possible to do something about evil without forcing other people to change. We can overcome the ancient illusion that it is necessary to do evil in order to produce good.

The question of identification

We have defined the cause of evil as identification with the localized self to the point of forgetting that we are more than this self, namely that we are non-local beings by nature. This identification has four levels:

• When people identify themselves with the physical body and their pier group (be it sex, race, ethnicity, nationality, religion, political affiliation or any other) they tend to believe that any threat (real or perceived) to their physical survival (or that of their group) warrants the killing or physical restraint of other people. It seems both necessary and justified to kill or control others in order to ensure your own survival (as you perceive it).

• When people identify themselves with emotions, their lives are controlled by fear-based emotions. They are constantly seeking to escape the unbearable fear that dominates their psyches, and almost anything becomes justifiable in order to achieve this goal. There are many examples of people who have killed in anger without thinking. We also see people who are so trapped in fear-based emotional patterns that they spend a lifetime seeking to control and manipulate others through the emotions.

• When people identify themselves with their thoughts and beliefs, they can fall prey to the idea that the ends can justify the means. They can come to believe that it is necessary to accomplish some overall goal of epic importance, such as converting all people to a particular religion or political ideology. They can believe this goal is so important that it overrides normal humanitarian concerns.

Killing six million Jews in concentration camps or killing 21 million people in order to defend Stalin's vision of communism becomes necessary means to an end. Because the analytical faculty is so good at filtering out information, no contradiction reaches the conscious mind. We also see people who are not willing to commit physical violence but who still spend a lifetime seeking to convince and convert others to their chosen thought system. Some of these people are willing to deceive and manipulate in order to accomplish their goal.

• When people identify themselves with or as the localized self, they automatically feel the fear of death. This fear is unbearable, and their entire lives revolve around doing the impossible: Overcoming the fear of death through the mortal self. The origin of the epic quest for some superior goal can be seen as a futile attempt to alleviate the fear of death by using the very mortal self that is the origin of this fear. It can never work, and we overcome the fear of death only by shifting our sense of identity to the non-local self. Only when we overcome the fear of death, can we fully respect both the free will of others and our own free will. We can then live our own lives while letting other people live theirs. We can live together without seeking to kill or control others and without letting others kill or control us.

The energy connection

Science has proven that everything is energy. This means every aspect of life has two components:

• There is a thought or idea that forms the matrix. One example is the thought matrix that defines what it means to be a Jew.

• There is the mental and emotional energy that people have colored through the thought matrix over time.

The combination of the thought matrix and the psychic energy forms a collective consciousness. When a child is brought up in a certain culture, it easily becomes overpowered by the psychic energy in the collective matrix. For example, if it was brought up in certain Arab societies, the child comes to hate Jews even though it might never have met a Jew.

Many other examples could be found. Over time, many people have contributed to building a collective consciousness of abusing alcohol. When a person opens his or her individual mind to the unbalanced use of alcohol, it will tie in to this collective momentum. The individual mind can become overwhelmed by the collective energy and that is why people quickly lose control. This also explains why millions of Germans were hypnotized by Adolph Hitler and did not awaken from the spell until the war was over. It explains why some Germans never awakened from the spell and why many other people remain hypnotized by some idea that denies our basic humanity.

By recognizing the importance of psychic energy, we open up the possibility that people can learn to identify and overcome the pull from these collective momentums. Awareness is the first tool, but others could be found. Many self-help techniques exist for releasing negative energy. This energy is created because our minds have the ability to take love-based energy and lower its vibration to that of fear. This means we can also learn to invoke and direct love-based energy into the energy stored in our individual energy fields and the collective field. Systematic techniques for doing this already exist, although they are beyond both the mainstream Christian and the materialistic mental boxes.

Knowledge is power

We now see that by developing a psychology of evil, we have opened up vast new opportunities for rising above evil on both the individual and the collective level. Why is there evil in the world? Because we have not so far been willing to look at and identify the psychological cause in all of us. Why is there *still* evil in the world? Because we have not been willing to take the knowledge available to us in the modern world and apply it to the problem of evil.

As we have seen, the psychological cause of evil is truly a sophisticated form of ignorance. We have never known more than we know today, and that means we have never had better opportunities for unmasking evil—in ourselves and on a larger scale. Doing this will require us to look beyond traditional mental boxes, for evil will seek to camouflage itself and hide behind anything that we are not willing to question. The willingness to question anything is the most powerful tool for overcoming evil.

In this book I have attempted to approach a psychology of evil by being as neutral and universal as possible. I have pointed out that we cannot understand evil without going beyond locality, and that means we are non-local beings. This naturally points to what has traditionally been seen as a spiritual or mystical outlook on life, yet I have avoided reference to specific philosophies or teachings. I have attempted to start with what is commonly known and what has been revealed by the most advanced branches of physics and psychology. Doing this has brought us forward, but it has not given us a complete understanding of evil as a phenomenon.

Many questions have not been answered or even addressed in this book. This will be done in the following books in the series, starting with *Cosmology of Evil*. In the second book, I will indeed go beyond traditional thought systems with the sole goal of seeking the most powerful explanations of evil that can be found. My only criteria will be: Can a theory explain something about evil that has not been explained by any previous theory? I will look at and expose the overall, cosmological cause of evil. That cause is still psychological but only when we go beyond the boundaries of mainstream psychology. I hope you will join me.